Paul Eade

walk & eat
STOCKHOLM

CONTENTS

This book is designed for short break walking holidays based in Stockholm, using public transport. The city is easily and inexpensively reached by several airlines. You have in your hand enough walks, excursions, restaurants and recipes to last two weeks — so you can pick and choose the most appealing.

Highlights at a glance

- 11 varied day walks, each with topographical map
- 2 fairly long excursions — one by train, one by boat
- 1 shorter part-day excursion, ideal for those with limited time
- a general overview of the extensive walks of the Sörmlandsleden — over a dozen waymarked hikers' trails in the national parks and forests south of Stockholm
- recommended restaurants, cafés and recipes
- hints on wheat-, gluten- and dairy-free eating in Sweden

INTRO

THE WALKS

Stockholm as a walking destination varies radically depending on the time of year that you visit. As a capital city, it's a year-round destination and you'll never be lost for something to do. But many outdoor activities are based on the summer holidays — and several cafés in the countryside follow suit, closing in winter. In addition, more ambitious walks can be dangerous and impassable in mid-winter — not to mention the biting cold.

We've therefore chosen mainly easy walks, most of which can be undertaken year-round. They range from flat rambles within or a few minutes from the city centre to hikers' walks in the forest and national parks. The book is designed for visitors using public transport. Of course, if you drive you may want to hire a car, but to be honest, it's not recommended. Firstly, parking in the city is extremely expensive and hard to find. Secondly, Sweden's drink driving laws mean you'll be over the limit after just one beer or a glass of wine — the limit is 20 mg of alcohol per 100 ml of blood — much stricter than in the UK for instance. And on the positive side, Stockholm's public transport system is little short of amazing. Even sparsely-populated areas are served by buses and trains usually running until late at night. Transport is usually punctual, modern, clean and reliable, with an easy to use journey planner (see page 14).

THE EXCURSIONS

Two long trips are outlined. First is to either or both castles at Gripsholm and Taxinge, near the town of Mariefred. This can be reached by regular inter-city train and then the heritage steam railway, Östra Södermanlands Järnväg, or by a relaxing cruise on veteran steamboat S/S Mariefred plying Lake Mälaren.

The second excursion is by boat through the Stockholm archipelago to the beautiful island of Grinda, where you can dine, walk, or even stay overnight in a traditional cottage.

For those with limited time, a third excursion — a short boat hop to the islands of Fjäderholmarna — will give you a taste of the archipelago.

THE RESTAURANTS AND CAFÉS

There are restaurants and cafés at the start, end and during many of the walks. But many away from the city are closed out of season (and sometimes in season!), so normally we suggest that you return to Stockholm for dinner — or perhaps make a local recipe yourself. For our featured restaurants a price guide is given, from £ (relatively inexpensive) to £££ (quite pricey). *No restaurant has paid, in cash or in kind, to be included in this guide.*

Unless you are camping, overnight accommodation can be thin on the ground away from the city, so apart from Grinda (see page 100), we suggest you sleep at a Stockholm base.

THE RECIPES

Most of the restaurants who shared recipes with us were happy to tell us the ingredients but preparation remained a 'secret' — so we have cooked all the recipes ourselves, to make sure that they work!

What we cannot guarantee, of course, is that they will taste as good back home as they did in Stockholm! So many factors come into play to make food taste better when you are on holiday, including the atmosphere and your appetite after a good walk, but also variety and quality of the products used. This is why we endorse self-catering (see page 10), so you can try out some of the recipes while you are in Stockholm.

Most of the Swedish recipes suggested are simple to prepare, based on a tradition using simple cooking facilities and making the most of limited ingredients during the harsh winters.

PLANNING YOUR VISIT
When to go

Stockholm is a city of extreme contrasts in the weather and you must take this into account before planning any visit.

The good news is that a large part of the year offers excellent walking weather. The **summer**, from around the beginning of June to mid-September, is often characterised by long, clear days, with almost unlimited daylight around mid-summer. Temperatures tend to be mild, but it can get hot, and visitors should also be prepared against mosquitoes and other biting insects — they love newcomers to the country. While the summer attracts its share of tourists, Stockholm is never full to bursting point, and the high season

Average city temperatures		
	Minimum	Maximum
Jan	-5°C/23°F	-1°C/30°F
Feb	-5°C/23°F	-1°C/30°F
Mar	-4°C/25°F	3°C/37°F
Apr	1°C/34°F	8°C/46°F
May	6°C/43°F	14°C/57°F
Jun	11°C/52°F	19°C/66°F
Jul	14°C/57°F	22°C/72°F
Aug	13°C/55°F	20°C/68°F
Sep	9°C/48°F	15°C/59°F
Oct	5°C/41°F	9°C/48°F
Nov	1°C/34°F	5°C/41°F
Dec	-2°C/28°F	2°C/36°F

Autumn is a good time to visit — for the calm and the colours.

is a fairly short affair, lasting from early July to mid-August. The ideal time to visit is June, when the countryside is coming into full bloom.

Be aware that midsummer (usually the third or fourth weekend in June) is a big national holiday in Sweden — at least as big as Christmas! While it can be fun to visit at this time, *be prepared for a national closedown,* including most restaurants and cafés.

The calm that descends from September makes **autumn** a good time to visit, but it does start to get chilly from mid-September — particularly in the evening, and the dark nights start drawing in. It can become bitterly cold from late October, when the first snows are possible, if rare. **Spring** is fresh, cheerful and often chilly, but note that April means still-lifeless parks, semi-frozen lakes and possible snowfall, sometimes heavy.

Winter offers a unique experience — but come prepared. A crystal-clear December day is magical, as are the lights and traditional build-up to Christmas. But walking opportunities in the countryside are limited. Nightfall comes at around 3pm in mid-winter, and temperatures rarely creep above zero (and can plummet to -15°C). Snow is a regular feature and many rural walks may be impassable or treacherous at best. Walking on a frozen lake can be a memorable experience but do not venture out on the ice unless you know what you are doing: currents and streams can make the ice unexpectedly thin, as many discover to their cost each year.

Getting there

Stockholm is very well served by **flights** from several parts of the UK and many European cities. Scandinavian Airlines (www.sas.se) is the national carrier; British Airways (www. britishairways.com) operates from Heathrow to Stockholm, while Danish carrier Sterling (www.sterling.dk) flies from Gatwick and East Midlands. Ryanair flies from Stansted, Liverpool, and Glasgow Prestwick plus several European airports to the outlying airports at Skavsta (Nyköping) and Västerås.

Travelling overland has become both attractive and in vogue again, due to congested airports and increased awareness of the 'carbon footprint'. It's a long haul to Stockholm, however. The best route from the UK is London-Brussels by Eurostar, overnight to Hamburg and then on to Copenhagen and finally to Stockholm — all in all about 22-23 hours. But bear in mind that 10 hours of this is on the Brussels-Hamburg sleeper; if two or more of you are travelling, a private cabin makes for a great way to travel, and of course it includes a night's sleep! Stockholm's national rail operator is SJ, www.sj.se.

It's also possible to travel by **ship** with Scandinavian Seaways (www.dfds.co.uk) from Newcastle to Bergen and then onward by **train** to Oslo and then Stockholm — a trip full of spectacular sights.

Where to stay

As one would expect of a European capital city, there is a wide range of **hotels** of all grades in Stockholm and around. If you want a bit of luxury, we suggest Hotel Rival (see page 49), in an excellent location on the south side of the city.

But if you don't want to splash out, it's really worth considering staying in an **apartment**. Generally, hotels in Stockholm tend to be of a very good standard, but you won't find rock-bottom prices as in many other countries. With an apartment you get the freedom, not afforded by a hotel, to cook your own meals, eat breakfast and sleep whenever you want. Quite a lot of private flats tend to be offered for rent during the summer; otherwise you could try Accome Hotel Apartments (www.accome.com) in Solna, Bromma or Kista. They are outside the city centre, but public transport links are swift, frequent and run late. The apartments are modern, with broadband, telephone, lounge, fully equipped kitchen and bathroom.

What to take

Pack simply. You definitely don't need to dress up in Stockholm when eating out or bar-hopping. With charges for hold luggage becoming more common with airlines, not to mention the various liquid restrictions and so on applied to hand luggage, packing for air travel has become a minefield. If you're going for a weekend, consider taking hand luggage only. This can save you *a lot* of queuing time, especially as it often enables you to check in on-line or at a self-service terminal at the airport, and you won't have to wait for baggage at the other end.

However, *always* check carefully the hand luggage allowances for the airline you are travelling with. Bear in mind that you *must not* exceed the hand baggage allowance or you may be denied boarding, and of course, you may well bring back home more things than you left with. If you want to avoid luggage and airport hassles, travel by train and/or ship!

No special equipment is needed for the walks but proper **walking boots** are preferable to any other footwear. Even on the simplest walks in this book you may encounter wet or stony terrain, while the Swedish winter weather will ruin ordinary shoes, even on the streets. A **sunhat** and high-protection **sun cream** are equally important; you may not think so, but there is a real risk of sunstroke on some walks, especially in June-August. **Insect repellent** is also a must during the Swedish summer — mosquitoes and other insects are commonplace and their bites can leave balloon-like lumps blowing up on your head, arms and legs. Each of you should carry a **rucksack**, so your load is shared. If you plan any walks off the beaten track, for instance any Sörmlandsleden (see page 134), then *all year round* it is advisable to carry a **first aid kit**, whistle, torch, spare socks and bootlaces and some warm clothing. If you're camping or staying in a cottage, don't forget torches! A long-sleeved shirt and long trousers should ideally be worn, for protection against the sun, mosquitoes and **ticks** (which can carry disease).

If you are coming to Sweden in **mid-winter** you will need *proper* winter clothing — not just UK 'winter' windcheaters and woollies; they won't be enough if it gets down to -12°C! A modern waterproof thick-lined winter jacket, really good gloves, hat, scarf, thick trousers and long johns and of course thick socks are all *essential.*

It is vital to carry **water** (at least half a litre, a litre in hot weather) with you on walks, even the shorter ones. Swedish tap water is of very high quality, so buying bottled water is a waste of money. Note that on the Sörmlandsleden and in the Tyresta National Park there may be no fresh water for long distances.

Planning your walks

All the walks and excursions are designed to be easily accessible by Stockholm's **excellent integrated public transport network** of buses, underground, local train and boats.

The walks have been **graded** for the deskbound person who nevertheless keeps reasonably fit. Our timings average 4km/ 2.5mi per hour on the flat, plus 20 minutes for every 100m/300ft of ascent. None of the walks involve sustained steep ascents or descents. Remember that these are simply *walking times;* increase the overall time by at least 50 percent, to allow for any breaks and nature watching. Several of the walks include historic sites and other points of interest — so what may be a two-hour walk in the book is often worth a whole day out!

Safety depends largely on knowing what to expect and being properly equipped. Most of the walks in this book are easily manageable and in areas where you will encounter other people, so it is perfectly safe to walk alone. Walk 11 (Tyresta) is, however, isolated in places, and the Sörmlandsleden can be *very* isolated, so it is advisable not to tackle these alone. All walks are easy to follow, with frequent signs and distinctive landmarks.

The walking **maps** are based on many sources, including the 1:50,000 'OS-style' 'Terrängkarta' (© Landmäteriets). But all of the routes have been heavily updated based on leaflets from various attractions and villages, as well as fieldwork.

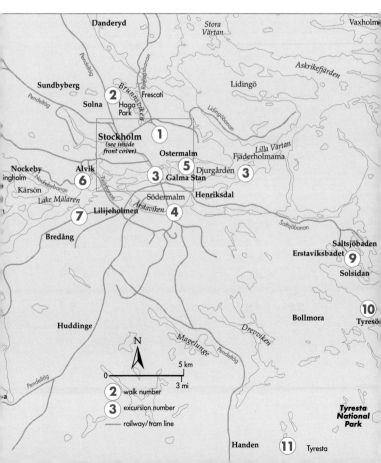

Verifying timetables in advance

While transport details are given in the 'logistics' panel at the start of each walk, remember that these timetables were correct at the time of writing. The best way to verify departures and returns is using the excellent journey planners available on the internet and/or by obtaining timetable booklets.

Buses, underground, tram and **local trains** are all operated by Storstockholms Lokaltrafik AB (www. sl.se); their **web site** includes a journey planner in English. The journey planner is very easy to use; here is an example based on Walk 2:

- click on 'In English' at the top
- at 'Journey Planner' click on 'Later'
- at 'From?', enter your starting point; this can be exactly where you are based, right down to the precise street address
- at 'To?' enter 'Frescati' (your destination station, the starting point for Walk 2)
- at 'When?' choose your date and departure time
- then click 'Search'

Now the departure times and connections for buses and trains will come up to view with arrival and journey times. You can click on 'Earlier', 'Later' and 'Return Journey' to explore more options. You can even click to see maps for your start, destination and whole route!

You may, of course, prefer to have **printed timetables** to hand. Booklets for all the bus, underground and local trains can be picked up for free at the '**SL Centers**'; in addition, all stations stock timetables for their route, and buses often have copies of their route timetable on board. **Timetable booklets** are produced separately:

- a booklet for each **underground** line — red, green and blue
- a booklet for each **local railway** line — pendeltåg (commuter train), Saltsjöbanan and Roslagsbanan
- a booklet for each **tram** route — Tvärbanan, Lidingöbanan and Nockebybanan
- booklets by area for all **buses**: in particular, make sure you pick up the 'Stockholms Innerstad' booklet, which contains all the central city bus routes, plus night buses and Djurgården tram and Djurgården ferry times.

The SL Centers are located at:

- T-centralen underground station, in the corridor leading from the railway station to the underground (open Mon-Sat- 06.30-23.15, Sun 07.00-23.15)
- Slussen, by the platform for the Saltsjöbanan trains (open Mon-Fri 07.00-18.00, Sat 10.00-17.00)
- Gullmarsplan, in the main hall of the transport interchange (open Mon-Thu 07.00-18.30, Fri 07.00-18.00, Sat 10.00-17.00)
- Tekniska Högskolan station, in the *tunnelbanan* entrance (open Mon-Fri 07.00-18.30, Sat 10.00-17.00)
- Fridhemsplan underground station (open Mon-Fri 07.00-18.30, Sat 10.00-17.00)
- Täby Centrum bus station (open Mon-Fri 07.00-18.30, Sat 10.00-17.00)

Inter-city trains, operated by SJ (www.sj.se), are only needed in the context of this book for the excursion to Gripsholm if you travel to Läggesta by train. SJ's web site also has a simple-to-use journey planner in English:

- click on 'In English' at the top right-hand side of the page
- at the section 'Buy Your Tickets', use the drop-down menu to choose 'Stockholm C' in the 'From' field. In the 'To' field, enter 'Läggesta' in 'Other locations' and click 'OK'.
- you now see a page where you choose the times and dates of travel using drop-down menus. Leave 'ticket type' blank for now and click 'continue'.
- on the next page you simply choose the number of passengers travelling (eg, 2 adults) and click 'continue.

Now about 6-7 departure times will come up with the possibility of choosing earlier and later departures as well. Now you select your ticket type:

- on the drop-down menu 'Choose here' you can select the type of ticket you want (it's only in Swedish but is easy to follow): '1 klass' is first class and '2 klass' is second class. You will also see 'just nu' options, which is for discounted advance-purchase tickets. It's unlikely that you'll save more than a few kronor with a 'just nu' ticket to Läggesta, but it's definitely something to think about if you are planning on travelling further afield — there are some real bargains to be had on the routes to Gothenburg and Malmö or to/from Oslo.
- when you have chosen the ticket you want by clicking the button for the specific train, click 'continue'.
- the next page simply deals with which type of seat you want, e.g. a table seat, from the drop down menu, and click 'continue'.
- the next page gives an overview and additional services, such as booking a taxi to/from the train, so normally you will simply click 'continue'.
- the next page is for payment method, which is most likely to be credit card. You can choose to 'collect tickets', which means you can pick up the tickets from the machines at Stockholm central station, using the code you will be given when you press 'continue'. Make a note of the code or fill in your email and/or mobile number to have the code sent to you.

You can of course book tickets in person at Stockholm central station. The staff are very helpful and speak very good English.

Ferries to different destinations around Stockholm and the archipelago are run by several different operators — see details under the excursions to Gripsholm, Grinda and Fjäderholmarna for the respective operators.

ON ARRIVAL
Local transport tickets and passes
Whichever airport you are coming from, or if you arrive by

train or coach, it's most likely that you'll end up at **Stockholm central station** [see town plan]. 'Centralen', as it is commonly known, is an integrated interchange for train, underground, long distance coaches and airport train and bus services.

If you are coming from the **main airport**, Arlanda, the choice of transport into the city is by the very rapid, but pricey Arlanda Express train* (www.arlandaexpress.com) or airport bus (www.flygbussarna.com). It's also possible to take a taxi, which is a cost-effective method if you are a group of three or four.

The outlying **'budget flight' airports at Västerås and Skavsta** are served by Flygbussarna airport bus, as is the **'city' airport** of Bromma.

Once at Centralen, follow signs to the underground *(tunnelbana)* and you will reach **SL's information and ticket counter**. But you can also buy a full range of local travel tickets at any of the '**Pressbyran**' shops, which also sell newspapers, magazines, food, drink and general items.

Tickets for **Storstockholmslokaltrafik (SL)** are available to suit every length of stay and travel demand. The system is integrated, so tickets are the same for local trains, underground, bus and tram. At the time of writing, the ticket system was undergoing a review (for about the third time in as many years!), so check on www.sl.se for the latest news.

The easiest ticket to buy is a single for the central zone,

*If you are travelling to northern Stockholm, you might also consider taking the Upptåget train (www.ul.se) one stop from Arlanda to Upplands Väsby, then continuing onwards by SL pendeltåg.

which is valid for an unlimited number of journeys for an hour but it's almost certain you'll want to travel extensively, so the best bet is to buy a **Travelcard**. These are available for 24 hours (from moment of purchase; 100kr), 72 hours (200kr), 7 days (260kr) and 30 days (690kr). The great news with travelcards is that not only will you have unlimited travel on all local trains, underground, buses and trams, but also on the heritage tram line from Norrmalmstorg to Djurgården and on the ferry from Slussen to Djurgården. What's more, the travelcard zones extend many kilometres outside the city; *transport to all the walks in this book is covered by a travelcard.*

Tourist information

Stockholm's **tourist information centre** is at Sverigehuset (Sweden house) at Hamngatan 27 in the city centre [1 on the plan]. It is open from 09.00-19.00 Mon-Fri, 10.00-17.00 Sat, 10.00-16.00 Sun. Here you can pick up plenty of free leaflets, maps and so on. They have an excellent, information-packed web site in English at www.stockholmtown.com. Another good source on the web for information about Sweden and Stockholm is www.sweden.se (Sweden's official web site). More informally, www.tripadvisor.com is a great resource for information from fellow travellers — just search for 'Stockholm' and take a dip into the site's forum.

Shopping for self-catering

Any apartment/aparthotel should have good quality kitchen-ettes with two-ring electric burners, a good-sized oven and tea-

Supermarket shopping list
washing-up liquid or
    dishwasher tablets
paper towels
aluminium foil
soap/shampoo
tissues/toilet paper
scouring pads
cleaning cloths
salt & pepper
herbs & spices
mineral water
milk
cream
yoghurt
coffee/tea/drinking chocolate
butter/cooking margarine
sugar
bread
fruit juice
soft drinks (see page 39)
wine/beer/cider (from
    Systembolaget)
cooking oil
salad oil & vinegar
eggs
tomato purée
rice/pasta
mayonnaise/mustard/sauces
travel wash
general purpose cleaner

and coffee-making facilities. You should also expect a decent selection of crockery and cutlery, but you might want to bring one or two of your own extra things.

It's worth having a little think about **everyday items** before you go. Items such as salt and sugar only come in big packs and although they're not expensive, it always seems a horrible waste to buy things like this for just a few spoonfuls' use. So if your stay is short you might want to bring some of these with you in small containers or bags. The same goes for general daily items such as shampoos and cleaning cloths, which nearly always come in bulk. Also a bottle of travel wash for laundry is a great little investment.

You'll need to visit a local **supermarket** to stock up on essentials and perhaps lots more. The hard fact is that good local food shops in Stockholm have been almost wiped out by supermarkets — you'll be lucky these days even to find an independent bakery (bageri) in your locality. If you don't want to buy your bread in the supermarket and can't find a *bageri,* some cafés double-up as bakeries, especially those called *'konditori'* (a tea/coffee shop that also sells breads and cakes).

The good news is that all the major supermarket chains have delicatessens, bakeries, butchers and fishmongers, and the quality is good. The main supermarket chains include ICA, Hemköp, Pris Extra, Willys and Coop. In addition, there are many smaller local Konsum shops, which have a wide range and pride themselves on quality but are a bit more pricey.

You'll notice a distinct lack of **alcohol** in the shops, with the exception of beer up to a strength of 3.5 percent. All store alcohol sales above this strength are confined to the much-discussed state-monopoly '**Systembolaget**' shops (www. systembolaget.se). In Stockholm a store should never be too far away, but bear in mind that if you go camping/self-catering on Grinda or Björkvik, *no off-licence sales of alcohol are available in the area.* Systembolaget shops are usually open from 10.00-18.00 Mon-Wed, 10.00-19.00 Thu-Fri and 10.00-15.00 Sat. They are always closed on Sundays and public holidays.

Sweden has a reputation for high alcohol prices, but at Systembolaget prices are reasonable (unless you want to buy spirits). So there's no need to lug drink with you to Sweden! Cans and bottles of beer cost from around 9kr each; wine from around 50kr a bottle. In the old days the drinks used to be in glass display cabinets and you made a note of the product number and took it to a counter to be served. A few of these stores survive, but most shops in Stockholm are now self-service. You'll find a good selection of wines and beers from around the world, with helpful and knowledgeable English-speaking staff.

Markets

The best general fruit and vegetable market is at **Hötorget** (Haymarket) in the city centre. Nearby [5 on the plan] is **Hötorgshallen** (www.hotorgshallen.se), one of three specialist

Christmas market at Gamla Stan

food halls in the city. Here you can find quality fish, breads, vegetables, spices and more, plus a Systembolaget. There are also four places to eat — from fast food to the more upmarket (and always popular) Kajsas Fisk, where they serve traditional Swedish fish dishes. Around 15 minutes' walk away, on Östermalm, is the **Saluhall** [4 on the plan], the city's most exclusive food market, shown on page 28. On Södermalm, visit **Söderhallarna** on Medborgarplatsen, a larger complex with shops, bars and cinemas, plus a gourmet food market in the basement (www. soderhallarna.com).

In December, you'll find **Christmas markets** in Gamla Stan (see overleaf) and at Skansen (see page 68). These are a *must*, with locally-produced foods and other products from all over Sweden in an unforgettably romantic atmosphere!

Introduction to Swedish food

Swedish cuisine is traditionally simple and sustaining. Long, hard winters meant that fresh vegetables were often in short supply; those that could be cultivated in harsh conditions were mainly root vegetables, such as potatoes and turnips.

Fish, particularly herring, has always been in plentiful supply, and is found everywhere — fresh, pickled or salted. **Meat** specialities are elk and reindeer; reindeer farming is a vital part of the economy of the Sami people in the north of Sweden.

Preserves are extremely popular, due to the wide availability of berries during the summer. Don't miss the sub-Arctic cloudberry, which is sold as a jam and also appears on dessert menus, often with ice-cream. Lingonberry jam is very popular as an accompaniment to meat or pancakes.

Vegetarians may find a surprisingly limited choice when eating out, although things are steadily improving. Sweden remains a predominantly meat-eating society, and if you say you are vegetarian it may be assumed that you eat fish. That said, eating establishments are coming round to the increasing vegetarian demand — particularly in Stockholm and other major cities, so there's often a vegetarian option on both lunch and dinner menus.

Swedes generally eat three meals a day. **Breakfast** usually consists of some form of bread, eaten with a topping such as cheese or ham, or cod roe caviar from a tube. Cereals — usually muesli or simple cereals such as corn flakes — are eaten with milk or *filmjölk,* a type of fermented milk a bit like yoghurt. It's not common to eat cooked food or toast at breakfast, though in winter porridge *(gröt)* is popular, taken with milk, jam and sugar. More traditional cafés serve breakfasts at very reasonable prices — including a simple sandwich, juice, tea or coffee and porridge.

Lunch is the traditional main meal of the day (see pages 24-25), and Swedes stop work to eat a proper cooked meal — they would not appreciate the British habit of eating sandwiches at the desk! A lighter **dinner** follows at home.

Coffee is drunk widely and at any time of the day; Sweden has one of the highest rates of coffee consumption per head in the world. Coffee was traditionally stove-boiled and nearly all lunch establishments include filter coffee in the price. Cafés in

Stockholm nowadays serve a wide range of coffees — from macchiato to latte, as in most modern European cities.

Tea is also popular, and Swedes go for a lot of different flavours, particularly fruit teas. Visit the **Tea Centre of Stockholm** (www.teacentre.se) at Horns-

gatan 46 [26 on the plan], where you can buy Söderblandning — the tea of south Stockholm, a blend of Chinese and Sri Lankan teas flavoured with tropical fruits and flowers. Beware, however: bearing in mind how much tea the Swedes drink at home, it is strange that café-bought tea is often a disappointment — you'll be lucky if you get anything more than a vastly overpriced cup, or even glass, of hot water and tea in a small infuser or a teabag (the worst case scenario being when milk is added to the water, preventing the tea from brewing).

Eating out and 'dagens lunch'

Make no mistake: dining out in Stockholm can burn a big hole in your pocket. Unlike southern Europe, Swedes don't tend to 'pop out' for dinner because they feel hungry — it's generally seen as a luxury. Many visitors baulk at the prices (particularly for main courses, which can often top the 200kr mark, and for wine — it's unlikely that you'll casually order a second bottle).

But help is at hand. The good news is that Swedes take lunch seriously and nearly always sit down to a full meal. In stark contrast to dinner, 'dagens lunch' offers deals that would be hard to beat anywhere. From as little as 55kr up to 85kr for something a little bit special, you are usually offered a main course, salad, bread, soft drink or low-alcohol beer, coffee or tea, and if you're really lucky, biscuits. It's normally a no-frills, canteen-type approach to the food (unless you go more up-market), and the salad can be anything from a few lettuce leaves to a hearty buffet plate. There's always a reasonable choice of mains — often one meat, one fish and a vegetarian option, usually pre-prepared to quickly serve impatient workers on their lunch break. Nevertheless, 'dagens lunch' offers traditional Swedish food at a very reasonable price.

Lunch tends to be an early affair; it's not unusual to see workers such as builders who have started early, tucking into meatballs at 10.30, and the office rush is well under way by 11.45. Most lunch establishments linger on until around 2.30pm or so, but if you arrive late, don't be surprised to see the most popular dishes wiped off the blackboard or be told they are 'slut' (sold out for the day). Note that drinking alcohol at lunchtime is still a bit of a no-no, except for the ubiquitous *lättöl,* light beer (thrown in with the meal), so expect raised eyebrows if you order something stronger at a lunch establishment. But attitudes are changing, albeit slowly, and it's common to see wine being drunk at the more up-market restaurants at lunchtime.

You won't have to wait to be fed in the evening; most restaurants are up and running at around 5pm, but don't leave it too late — after 10pm you'll be struggling to find anywhere open. For budget eating in the evening, pubs and bars are an option.

Starting at Stockholm's most exclusive food market, this walk gives a taste of life in the capital, including some of the city's parks. Our destination is Haga Park, one of the finest — a stroller's paradise and home to many interesting and unusual features.

city centre and haga park

WALK

1

Start out at **Östermalmstorg underground station**: take the exit at the centre of the platform, marked 'Nybrogatan'. Follow the signs to the exit on Nybrogatan. Coming out of the station, turn left. Directly ahead of you, to the right across Humlegårdsgatan, is **Östermalms Saluhall** [4 on the plan inside the front cover]. Built in 1888, this is Stockholm's outstanding market hall (www. saluhallen. com). It retains its original character and is home to over 20 traders selling almost all the quality ingredients you could wish for — meat, cheeses, seafood, bread, fruit, vegetables, desserts and coffee. It also houses two fish restaurants, a bistro, sandwich bar, sushi bar and coffee bar.

Distance: 7km/4.3mi; 2h15min

Grade: easy; on well-maintained paths throughout, with no steep gradients and walkable at any time of the year. See the plan inside the front cover to begin.

Equipment: see pages 10-12; sun protection

Transport: U red line from Centralen to Östermalmstorg (journey time 2min; frequent service); return on 🚌 59 from Haga Forum to Centralen (journey time 21min; buses every 10min weekdays, every 20min Sat/Sun — some buses continue beyond Centralen to Slussen and Norra Hammarbyhöjden).

Refreshments: numerous cafés en route through the city; Simons Skafferi for lunches or prepared picnics; two cafés in Haga Park

Points of interest:
Saluhall food market
Humlegården
Eriksbergsplan
City library (Stadsbibliotek) and park
Haga Park

Leaving the Saluhall by the Humlegårdsgatan exit, turn left and walk down the hill. After crossing Sturegatan, you will see **Humlegården** on your right. This city park is home to the **Kungliga Bibliotek** (Swedish Royal Library) — the national

Östermalms Saluhall, where the walk begins

archive library, where all domestic printed materials in Swedish are collected. At the end of Humlegårdsgatan the road meets Birger Jarlsgatan, one of the longest streets in central Stockholm. Turn right and walk along Birger Jarlsgatan, which nearly always retains a calm atmosphere despite its central location and is one of the more unspoilt major central streets. When the street comes to a multiple junction you are at **Eriksbergsplan**, with a huge wheel-type sculpture 'Fordon' (Vehicle) by K J Bejemark. This was also the area that in the 19th century was home to the city's public punishments.

Carry on along Birger Jarlsgatan until you reach a fork, where Roslagsgatan goes straight ahead. To the right is a nice little urban park, **Jarlaparken**. At this point cross Birger Jarlsgatan and turn left up Rehnsgatan. Near the beginning of the street, on the right, is Simons Skafferi [23 on the plan], which specialises in high-quality take away food (see page 32).

Walk to the end of Rehnsgatan, where it meets Sveavägen,

the busiest road in the city centre. Crossing the road you come to a park and the unmistakable rotunda that houses the **Stads-bibliotek** (Stockholm City Library). The park was designed in conjunction with the library, built by Gunnar Asplund in 1928, to give a sense of space around the building. Walk along Sveavägen towards the library and pop inside to see the remarkable rotunda. The library's collection of English-language books would put many British city libraries to shame!

Now carry on along Sveavägen to its end, at Sveaplan. Go straight on, using the pedestrian crossings, and take the pedestrian underpass beneath the road complex. Coming out on the far side, carry straight on along the path, keeping to the right of the distinctive **Wenner-Gren Center**, a centre for scientific exchange. You now leave the city behind. Follow the path around the back of the centre and walk under the **railway bridge**. Shortly after this, turn left (a right turn leads to Walk 2). Keeping the water of Brunnsviken on your right, follow the path by the water's edge past the restaurant/café on your left and then some tennis courts.

You now come into the southern edge of **Haga Park**. Developed in the late 18th century by King Gustav III, Haga is a fine example of what Swedes call an 'English park' — based on nature, with winding paths and woodland, and scattered buildings providing constant new and surprising experiences.

Just beyond the tennis courts, take the path to the right that leads slightly uphill into an oak forest. As the path bends around to the left through the trees, you come out into a more open area with a small, simple café. The path then nears

Copper
Tents
Ruins
Castle
Echo
Temple
Pavillion

*Haga
Park*

E4

Haga
Forum

E4/E20

Brunnsviken

Universitetet

Laduviken

N

0   0.5 mi

0.5 km

Bellevue
Park

*See town plan
for the first
half of the walk*

Vasastaden

Karlberg

Karlberg

Karlbergssjön

Stadshagen

Kungsholmen

Norrmalm

Österma

Östermaln

Österma

Brunnsviken on the right and a **cliff face** on the left, where there is a grotto — the remains of a once-planned system to pump water into a reservoir above the rocks. Next, on the right, you see **Gustav III's Pavilion** across the water. Where the water ends, follow the path around to the right, to the other side of water, to

The Ekotemplet

walk to this pavilion (guided visits only) and just beyond this the **Ekotemplet** (Echo Temple).

Retrace your steps to where you doubled back near the water. Now walk straight ahead across the huge lawn to the **copper tents**. Built by Louise Jean Desprez between 1787 and 1790, these copper-clad buildings were designed to give the illusion of a sultan's encampment at the edge of the forest. The middle tent houses the **Haga Park Museum**, the one to the east a café/restaurant. Facing the tents, walk to the left: this higher path swings back round towards where you started into the park. Now pine trees offer a contrast to the usual park foliage.

When you come back to the **park's south gates**, walk straight on and you will come to the modern buildings of **Haga Forum**. Turn right on the road here. Walk past the bus stop for buses to the airport; about 40m/yds further on is the stop for bus 59, with frequent services into central Stockholm.

Simons Skafferi

A café, take-away and delicatessen. Emphasis on modern Swedish and European dishes and organic food. Lunches to eat in or take away, plus prepared picnics. Simon Skafferi's philosophy is that 'food and drink are, in every way, life'; he believes in 'the old-fashioned, almost-forgotten ideal of eating with the family'.

With this in mind, Chris and Simon at the Skafferi prepare food with love and imagination. You can drop by for a coffee or to buy quality organic food and ingredients. There are also wine-tasting events.

We've included two recipes from Simons Skafferi in this book — a Västerbotten cheese quiche (see page 93) and the fish and seafood stew shown opposite. Fish stew is a staple on Swedish menus, particularly in winter, and it's often a good-value dish in restaurants. *Aïoli* is almost always included — either a dollop on the stew or on the side to add as you wish.

SIMONS SKAFFERI
Kungstensgatan 12, Stockholm (also lunch restaurant and café at Kungstensgatan 2)
(08 612 38 40; www.simonsskafferi.se £

8 main courses, including fish and seafood soup with saffron; chicken stew with coconut milk and tomato, served with grilled vegetables and rice or red quinoa; Västerbotten pie; smoked salmon and spinach lasagne.

snacks: coffee and bagel; various smoothies

walkers' special: picnic package in cooler bag, with starter, main course, dessert and water

---

restaurants

eat

SIMON SKAFFERI'S FISH AND SEAFOOD STEW

Heat the bouillon and wine in a large pan. Add the mussels and simmer until the shells open. Take the mussels out of the bouillon and remove the shells.

Add the cream and tomato purée. Lightly fry the butter with the saffron and blend into the bouillon. Cut the vegetables into large chunks and cook in the bouillon for 10 min. Then add the curry powder.

Cut up the fish and add to the bouillon, cooking for no more than 10 min. The final touch is to add the mussels and prawns or crayfish *just before serving*.

To make the aïoli, crush the garlic, add the egg yolks and lemon and mix into a paste. Add the oil a little at a time with frantic whisking, to make a well-blended, thick, creamy sauce. Add salt and pepper. Keep cold until serving. OR simply crush the garlic with the salt and pepper, and then stir into a really good, bought mayonnaise.

For the croutons, heat the oven to 190°C, 375°F, gas mark 5. Place the bread cubes on a buttered oven tin. Drizzle olive oil over them and cook for 3-4 min.

Ingredients (for 4 people)
500 g fresh fillet of firm
   white fish (cod if possible)
400 g mussels in their shells
225 g prawns or crayfish
800 ml fish bouillon
2 whole fennel
2 red or yellow peppers
1 leek
2 level tsp curry powder
pinch saffron
400 ml cream
1 tsp finely chopped dill

For the aïoli
3 garlic cloves
2 egg yolks
300 ml olive oil
pinch sea salt
pinch black pepper

For the croutons
white bread (crusts removed
   and cut into cubes)
olive oil

recipes

eat

The stunning Bergius Botanic Garden and the peaceful waters of Brunnsviken are the highlights of this walk (which can easily be combined with Walk 1). But why not make a day of it, calling in at the two museums which lie en route?

2

brunnsviken

WALK

Alighting on the wooden platform at the small station at **Frescati**, you can see the **Swedish Museum of Natural History** (www.nrm.se) in the large building in the near distance across the railway tracks; it's just a five-minute diversion if you wish to visit.

Otherwise, walk along the platform in the same direction as the departing train and, at the end of the platform, turn left. You come straight to the entrance to the **Bergianska Trädgården** — the Bergius Botanic Garden (www.bergianska.se). Entrance to the open air parts of the garden is free.

The garden's origins date back to the 18th century, but it

Distance: 5km/3.1mi; 1h30min

Grade: easy; mostly on well-maintained paths, walkable all year round. There are a couple of very short steep sections by Brunnsviken, which may be difficult in winter.

Equipment: see pages 10-12; sun protection

Transport: U red line to Tekniska Högskolan (journey time 6min; frequent service), then local Roslags-banan 🚃 from Stockholms Östra (Stockholm East) station to Frescati (journey time 4min; trains every 30min or every 20min at peak times). Return on any of several 🚌 from Sveaplan to Stockholm city centre.

Refreshments: cafés in Bergianska Trädgården

Points of interest:
Swedish Museum of Natural History
Bergianska Trädgården
Carl Eldh Museum
Bellevue Park

was moved to its current location in 1885. Walk straight ahead and soon you will see the main buildings of the garden on your left — the **Gamla Orangerie** (orangery) and the **Edvard Anderson Conservatory**. The Orangerie houses a café selling light meals and snacks (open daily from late May to the end of September, 11.00-16.00). The Conservatory (admission charge

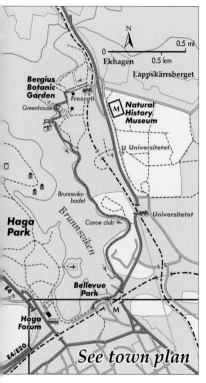

50kr) was opened in 1995 from money bequeathed by Edvard Anderson to create a Mediterranean winter garden; it is open year-round from 11.00-17.00 daily and also has a simple counter serving drinks and cakes.

Coming out of the conservatory and turning left, you pass various open-air herb gardens and a pond before reaching the **Victoria Greenhouse** (admission 20kr, open May-September, 11.00-16.00 weekdays, 11.00-17.00 weekends), with its stunning displays of water lilies amongst other plants.

You are now very close to the water of **Brunnsviken**. Coming out of the Victoria Greenhouse and turning left, there is an area with picnic tables and an Italian terrace, all with views over the water to Haga Park on the far side.

Standing right beside the water, take the path to the left, to stroll along the water's edge. The path is mostly easy, but there are one or two slightly tricky descents (with helpful steps or railings). The path runs past **Brunnsviksbadet** (a bathing area) and **Brunnsvikens canoe club**. Carry on as the path makes a U-bend to the right, and you can see across the water to where you started out. The buildings seen inland belong to the university. When the path meets a main road (Roslagsvägen), turn right, still on the path, and follow it past a **marina** and through a wooded area, with a bank to your left.

When you reach a path going left, you could join Walk 1 by keeping straight ahead beside the water and picking up the notes for Walk 1 on page 29 (see text from just after the 'railway bridge'). Otherwise, turn left along this short path and then left again along Brunnsviksvägen. Where the road forks, go right up Lögebodavägen and over the **railway footbridge**. The road twists and climbs briefly before reaching the **Carl Eldh Museum** on the left (www. eldhsatelje.se). Carl Eldh was a Swedish artist and sculptor, and his sculptures are dotted around Stockholm — you will pass one or two of them on Walk 6.

Eldh lived in this building, which was also his studio; from

Carl Eldh's sculpture of the celebrated Swedish author, August Strindberg

here he could take advantage of fine views across Brunnsviken and Haga, as well as the light and calm parkland atmosphere. Stop for a moment and take it all in for yourself. Unfortunately, at the time of writing the museum was closed — a tunnel is being blasted for a road directly underneath the museum. Because of possible heavy vibrations, the sculptures have had to be removed and it is not known when the museum will re-open. Check the web site, which has an English version, for the latest update on the situation.

Retrace your steps back down the hill until you reach Bellevuevägen on your left. Now referring to the town plan inside the front cover, follow this through lovely **Bellevue Park** and keep by the perimeter of the **Wenner-Gren Center** buildings on your right. Staying by the buildings, you come to an underpass, which takes you out onto Sveaplan and Sveavägen.

From here there are **buses** back into the city centre, or you might follow Walk 1 in reverse (see the town plan), to walk past the Stockholm City Library. If you like, you can continue down Sveavägen to **Hötorget** in the city centre. If you do so, you can visit **Adolf Frederiks Church** [23 on the plan], on the right-hand side of the road between the Rådmansgatan and Hötorget underground station entrances. Sweden's former prime minister, Olof Palme, is buried in the churchyard here. If you cross Sveavägen at the junction with Olof Palmes Gata, just outside the underground station entrance is the spot where Palme was assassinated on 28 February 1986. It is marked by a plaque in the ground and flowers are sometimes laid there.

SWEDISH SOFT AND LOW-ALCOHOL DRINKS

Sweden has long had an uneasy relationship with alcohol. Historically, Sweden is part of the 'vodka belt', with spirits sometimes drunk in large quantities. *Brännvin* (literally 'burn wine') was distilled from grain and potatoes, and as Sweden became rapidly industrialised and urbanised in the late 19th century, its consumption caused widespread health and social problems. A referendum on the prohibition of alcohol was held in 1922. While it was defeated by the narrowest of margins (49% in favour, 51% opposed), a rationing system, *motbok*, was nevertheless put in place until 1955. Today, beverages containing more than 3.5% alcohol are only available through the government monopoly, **Systembolaget**, and may only be sold to those aged 20 and over (although, paradoxically, the minimum age for purchase in bars is 18).

While attitudes towards alcohol are slowly coming into line with other parts of Europe, the temperance movement remains strong. Drinking at 'dagens lunch' (see page 25) is certainly taboo for those at work. This has in turn led to Sweden having an imaginative variety of soft and low-alcohol drinks as an alternative, and these are also consumed on festive occasions. While the domination of the large soft-drink manufacturers has threatened the very existence of some of these traditional drinks, there has also been a recent revival — they are being sold as quality products by specialist small producers, particularly in rural areas where the tradition is strongest.

You'll find *lättöl* (light beer) on offer at almost every 'dagens lunch' establishment, plus virtually all bars and restaurants. A licence is not needed to serve *lättöl,* which cannot exceed 2.25% alcohol, so it's also sold in cafés. *Lättöl* is an unremarkable brew, but works well enough to wash down a meal.

Much more interesting, though sadly harder to find outside

the shops, is *svagdricka* (literally 'weak drink') — a sweetened, low-alcohol, malty stout-type beer, similar to the *kvass* consumed in Russia and Eastern Europe. Formerly a common drink with meals, *svagdricka* almost disappeared in the 1970s, but has been revived by specialist brewers.

From left to right: *Champis*, fruit 'champagne', two types of *svagdricka*, and *påskmust*

By far the most popular Swedish special soft drink is *must.* It was created in 1910 by Harry Roberts and his father Robert as a non-alcoholic alternative to beer. Roberts AB of Örebro exclusively make the syrup for the drink; the exact recipe is a closely-guarded secret, but it consists of carbonated water, citric acid, spices and other flavourings, plus malt and hops extract to give it a 'beery' taste. *Must* is mainly drunk at Christmas *(julmust),* when it accounts for 50 percent of soft drink sales in December. It also appears at Easter as *påskmust,* but is hard to find at other times of the year — although in 2007 a version called *sommarmust* was produced. The content is the same for all versions. *Must* can be aged if stored in glass, and aficionados sometimes buy it in December for drinking 12 months later.

Champis and *Pommac* are non-alcoholic alternatives to sparkling wine. *Pommac,* originally made as an alternative to wine for the upper classes, is made from fruits and berries and is aged in oak casks for three months. In 2004 it was announced that sales of *Pommac* would cease, but the decision was met with outrage and a 50,000-strong petition, and it was soon back on the shelves.

There are also various other carbonated fruit drinks, traditional favourites including Trocadero and Portello, and you will also see *saft* (fruit cordial) for sale in supermarkets and cafés (where it is sometimes provided free with lunch).

JANSSONS *FRESTELSE*

Janssons *frestelse* (Jansson's temptation) is a traditional Swedish casserole dish made of potatoes, onion, anchovies and cream. It can be eaten as a dish in itself, and it often appears at the Swedish Christmas smorgasbord. The origins of the recipe are uncertain.

Some say it was named after Pelle Janzon, a food-loving Swedish opera singer from the 19th century. However, there has also been a strong case made that the name was taken from a 1929 film, *Janssons Frestelse*, and that its use spread after it was presented at a society dinner.

Peel the potatoes and cut them into long, thin slices. Chop the onion coarsely. Place half the potatoes in a buttered oven-proof dish. Add the onion and the anchovy fillets (don't discard the anchovy liquid). Add the rest of the potatoes, cover with bread-crumbs and add the butter in small pieces. Pour the anchovy liquid and half of the cream over the mixture.

Bake the dish in the oven at 225°C, 425°F, gas mark 7 for 50 min-1 h. Add the rest of the cream after it has cooked for 30 min.

Ingredients (for 4 people)
8 medium-sized potatoes
1 large onion
1 tin of anchovy fillets
  (approximately 125 g)
30 g butter
200-300 ml single
  cream/cooking cream
  (matgrädde)
6-1/2 tbsp breadcrumbs
salt
white pepper

recipes

eat

A city walk which opens up the delights of the Söder-malm district of Stockholm — the most lively part of the inner city, offering everything from eating, drinking and shopping to fascinating architecture, views and nature. The walk takes a diversion into the Old Town, one of the city's most popular areas among visitors.

södermalm and the old town

WALK

The walk starts at **Mariator-get**, in the heart of **Södermalm**. This area was formerly the main working-class district of the city, and it retains a strong identity of its own — expressed through sport and popular culture. Nowadays 'Söder' offers the widest range of eating and drinking establishments in the city, with everything from locals' bars to Gondolen (see page 60).

Arriving at Mariatorget, take the exit towards the front of the train, past the sculpture 'Man and Pillar' by Asmund Arle and up the lift to Torkel Knutssongatan. Turn right out of the exit and follow the road to Hornsgatan. Cross this and

Distance: 5km/3mi; 2h+

Grade: easy, mainly on well-maintained, easily followed routes. But take care on Montelius Vägen, parts of which can be treacherous in winter. Use the plan inside the front cover for most of the walk.

Equipment: see pages 10-12; walking sticks; sun protection.

Transport: U red line from Centralen to Mariatorget (journey time 5min); return via green line from Medborgarplatsen (journey time 4min); frequent trains on both lines

Refreshments: numerous cafés, bars and restaurants en route

Points of interest:
Montelius Vägen
Mariatorget
Maria Magdalena Church
Old Town (Gamla Stan)
Gondolen
Katarina Church

continue along the road until it merges into Bastugatan on the right. Follow Bastugatan up the slope and around to the right. Just around the bend you will see an opening between the buildings to your left marked '**Kattgränd**'. Take this and walk down the steps onto the footpath known as **Montelius Vägen**. Follow this to the right (it can be very slippery here in winter). After about 80m/yds the path becomes a wooden platform and opens out onto spectacular views across Riddarfjärden across to Stadshuset and the Old Town. About halfway along the platform, through a small gate on the right, there are plenty of tables and seats for a break in **Ivar-Los Park**. The park, a very popular locals' picnic spot, is named after Ivar-Lo Johansson, the prolific proletarian novelist.

Just beyond the park, there is a gap to the right, marked 'Bläcktornsgränd'. Take this path and follow it back to the residential area. Good-value Café Lucas is to your right — a little hidden gem that also hosts small art exhibitions; perhaps stop for a coffee at one of their outdoor tables. Continue down the slope and steps, passing between the old residential streets of Tavasgatan and Brännkyrkagatan. The path joins the road and slopes steeply back down to Hornsgatan.

As you come out onto Hornsgatan, with the Black and Brown pub to your left, you will see **Mariatorget square** across the road. There are some cafés and bars in the area, notably Rival (see page 49). The square's centrepiece is a fountain featuring a sculpture of Thor slaying a dragon (see page 42).

Back on Hornsgatan and turning left from Bläcktornsgränd, Hornsgatan continues towards Slussen. Take the footpath rising on the left to what is known as **Hornspucken**, where there are several commercial art galleries and the Stockholm Tea Centre (see page 24). On the other side of the road is **Maria Magdalena**, Södermalm's oldest church, dating from 1625.

Continuing along Hornsgatan you come to a junction, with Gondolen looming in front of you and the **Stadsmuseum** (City Museum, well worth a visit) at the start of Götgatan to the right.

View from Montelius Vägen on Södermalm across to Kungsholmen

If you follow the pavement to the left you will find yourself on Södermalmstorg. Cross over the underground tracks below you and, with the water to your left, follow the road, Katarinavägen. When you come to the traffic lights, cross the road and then cross again at the adjoining set of lights. You are now at Järntorgsgatan, which leads into the **Old Town** (**Gamla Stan**).

Dating back to the 13th century, there is no escaping the Old Town's charm — but it can become overwhelmed with tourists, espe-

Street in the Old Town

45

Katarina Church

cially in summer. It comes into its own at night, particularly in winter, when the streets are deserted and evoke past times.

Järntorgsgatan leads to Järnstorget: cross this square to Österlånggatan. This is away from the main tourist drag and includes, at number 51, Den Gyldene Freden, a restaurant whose interior is little altered since 1722. Further up Österlånggatan, turn up the slope to your left, Köpmanbrinken; then go left again along Köpmangatan, where there are craft shops and the like. At the end of Köpmanbrinken is **Stortorget**, the Old Town's main square.

Doubling back from Köpmangatan to Köpmanbrinken, turn left, back onto Österlånggatan. At the end of this street is Slottsbacken at the side of the **Royal Palace** — a tourist magnet, but with reasonably priced admission at 90kr.

Walking down the hill on Slottsbacken, you come to Skepps-bron; in front of you the waters of **Strömmen**. Cross the main road and turn left along the quay. Walking along here you can see across the water to Skeppsholmen and, further away, the docking points for ferries to Finland. Keep to the quayside until you reach the departure area for the ferry to Djurgården on your left. Walk up the steps just beyond here: ahead now is the landmark Gondolen complex — a huge elevated platform with the Gondolen restaurant at the top. The Katarina lift (cost 10kr) whisks you straight up to the top where there is an open-air platform with breathtaking views. (See more about the lift and restaurant on pages 60-61).

The platform leads directly out to Mosebacke, Södermalm's cultural centre, with a theatre/concert/nightclub venue, plus a restaurant where meals are served outdoors in summer (in winter there's a wonderful buffet brunch with live jazz). It is also home to one of the city's most beautiful squares, **Mose-backe Torg**. Walking round the edge of the square, past the theatre and a water tower, you come to Östgötagatan. Follow this street to the right down the hill (perhaps diverting to **Katarina Church** with its attractive grounds on your left).

Mosebacke Torg

Cross busy Folkungagatan. You are now officially in the area that has recently been dubbed 'SoFo' (South of Folkungagatan) — one of the trendiest, liveliest and most bohemian areas of Stockholm. From here on refer to the map overleaf. Östgötagatan meets Skånegatan, where there are shops, café/bars and restaurants.

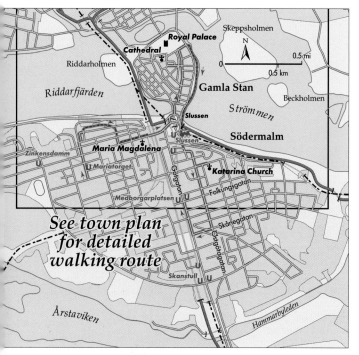

Following Skånegatan to its westwards extent, you come out on the main road of Götgatan. Turn right and you soon come to several entrances for **Medborgarplatsen underground station**. You may also want to take a look at **Medborgarplatsen** — literally 'the citizen's square', known locally as 'Medis' — where there are open-air bars in summer and a small skating rink in winter.

Hotel Rival

Hotel Rival is a boutique hotel in the heart of Södermalm. Rival is the result of the vision of its owner, Benny Andersson (formerly of ABBA), to create a hotel and venue with style and glamour. We're not biased – Rival really is hard to beat. Not only is it cool and stylish, but it's much more than a hotel. It has a large cinema, bakery and café — so even if you're not staying, be sure to visit.

Rival's cocktail bar is always popular and often has events at weekends with DJs. The restaurant is perfect for a treat — in spring and summer there is an outdoor balcony overlooking beautiful Mariatorget Square.

HOTEL RIVAL
Mariatorget 3 (**08 545 789 00**
www.rival.se

menu with a definite Swedish flavour

8 starters, including the Swedish classic *toast skagen* (shrimps in mayonnaise, dill and kalix bleak roe on toast)

10 main dishes — varying with the seasons but always including veal pattie à la Wallenberg with potato purée, lingonberries, garden peas and browned butter.

always a **vegetarian dish** — like grilled goat's cheese with vegetables, mixed salad and rosemary honey

10 different desserts — such as cheesecake from Småland with cloudberries and cream

restaurants

eat

Snotty

If you're after somewhere with a bit of edge, but where you can also eat quality food, Snotty is the place to be.

Located in the heart of Stockholm's hip 'SoFo' district, Snotty is *always* busy with a crowd of all ages. The bar's decoration is based around new wave and alternative music from the 70s and 80s, and different DJs play from 21.00 Wednesdays to Saturdays — anything from Swedish indie to French kitsch pop.

Swedish meatballs (recipe opposite)

SNOTTY
Skånegatan 90 (08 644 39 10
Open daily 17.00-01.00... £-££

one of the few places where you have the choice for a **full meal** at the table or a **simple bar snack**

menu changes constantly, but **Swedish meatballs** are a staple

restaurants

eat

SWEDISH MEATBALLS

Different meatball recipes are countless, but as a general rule *köttbullar* (meatballs) in Sweden are made with ground beef or a combination of ground beef and pork, mixed with breadcrumbs soaked in milk and finely chopped onions. They are seasoned with white pepper or allspice and salt. Swedish meatballs are usually served with boiled or mashed potatoes and lingonberry jam. Traditionally, gravy is common, though its popularity has lessened in more modern cuisine.

Peel and grate the onion, and lightly beat the egg. Mix the breadcrumbs with the cream and leave for a few minutes to soften. Add the meat, onion, spices and egg and mix well. Form the mixture into round balls, about 2.5 cm thick.

Melt the butter in a large frying pan over a medium heat. Add half the meatballs and fry until browned. Set those aside and repeat the procedure with the remaining meatballs.

Mix the sugar and beef stock. Return the first batch of meatballs to the pan and pour over the stock. Increase the heat and boil vigorously for a few minutes, turning the meatballs from time to time, until the liquid is reduced to a syrup and the meatballs are thoroughly cooked.

Serve with new potatoes or mashed potatoes and lingonberry jam.

Ingredients (for 6 people)
75 g breadcrumbs
100 ml single cream/cooking cream *(matgrädde)*
200 g minced pork
400 g minced beef
1 small onion
1/2 tsp allspice
1/2 tsp ground cloves
pinch ground nutmeg
1 medium free-range/organic egg
20 g butter
2 tbsp brown sugar
150 ml beef stock

recipes

eat

This walk from Zinkensdamm to Henriksdal is very popular with locals. Its easy access makes it a perfect city walk all year round, while there are many places for refreshment stops in summer. You will be beside the water for most of the way, enjoying terrific views.

årstaviken

WALK

Start the walk at the only exit from **Zinkensdamm underground station**. You come out on Ringvägen and cross Hornsgatan — at the heart of the 'authentic' **Södermalm**, with its working-class atmosphere, local shops and good-value bars and restaurants. After crossing Hornsgatan, continue along Ringvägen. On the right you cannot miss **Zinkensdamm Sports Stadium**, the home of Hammarby Bandy Club. Bandy, which has its origins in the UK, is basically field hockey played on ice, using a small, bright orange-coloured ball. Hammarby play bandy from November to April, and if you can bear standing on concrete terraces in sub-zero temperatures for nearly two hours, the games make for very lively and vocal entertainment!

At the end of the outer wall of the stadium, take the first

Distance: 7km/ 4.3mi; 2h30min

Grade: easily followed walk on well-maintained paths. A good walk for any time of the year, although the paths around Tantolunden Park can be treacherous in winter.

Equipment: see pages 10-12; walking sticks; sun protection

Transport: **U** red line from Centralen to Zinkensdamm (journey time 6min, frequent service). Return from Henriksdal to Slussen on Saltsjöbanan light ⬛ (journey time 5min; trains every 20min) or local 🚐 (very frequent buses).

Refreshments: Café Tubby and Café Nyfiken Gul (both mid-way), Café Fåfängen (at the end), Café Loopen Marin (on the alternative walk). Other small cafés/kiosks en route — all closed in winter.

Points of interest:
Zinkensdamm Sports Stadium
Tantolunden Park
Årstaviken
Stockholm Transport Museum
Fåfängen

Alternative walk: Zinkensdamm–Skanstull–Gullmarsplan–Zinkensdamm circuit. 11km/ 6.8m; 3h30min. Circular walk taking in both shores of Årstaviken. See walking notes on page 58.

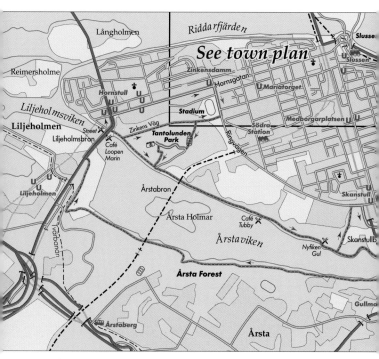

path to the right, Zinkens Väg. Follow this and you enter **Tantolunden Park**. The park is noted for its 'colony' of small cottages
and gardens/allotments. After around 50m/yds, follow the
path to the left and cross a gravel **football pitch**. At the other
side of the pitch you join a small road, Tantolundsvägen. Follow
this uphill to the right, with chalets to your left. The road
widens as it ends, where there are some seats at a fine

viewpoint. From here you can see across to the southern suburbs of Stockholm and immediately below you, the waters of Årstaviken.

With your back to the viewpoint, start to retrace your steps; then take the wooden steps down to the right. These lead to another area of chalets and gardens — a sea of colour in summer. Now follow the path to the left and then down the next set of steps. Ahead of you are **two large bridges** (**Årstabron**) that take the railway across Årstaviken. Follow the path towards these, down to the water's edge. Then head left, walking under both bridges.

Now follow the path beside the waters of **Årstaviken**. During the summer a 'reggae café', Café Tubby, is open, serving light snacks and playing reggae sounds in a very laid-back atmosphere. Eventually the path opens out as you pass a maintenance area for boats, then swings round past another open-air café, Nyfiken Gul. This offers very good-value grilled food and is licensed.

One of the colourful cottages in Tantolunden

Past Nyfiken Gul you approach **another set of bridges** that carry the road and underground railway over Årstaviken. Stay close to the water *(but for the Alternative walk divert here; see page 58).* Walk under the bridges and past a **lock** for the boats. Beyond here the scenery changes dramatically. The area by the water becomes built up and the path takes a dog-leg into **Hammarby Hamnen**. Here on the northern side there are several new and some older flat developments, and the path opens out into a dockside. On the far side of the water there is a huge amount of work taking place for new residential areas.

This area offers an interesting insight into Stockholm's 1950s housing developments, with the carefully-planned parks of **Vintertullsparken** and **Barnängsparken**. Just after the latter, there is a small kiosk/café, called Kajsa's. Opposite is a **boat terminal**, both for free ferries to the other side of the water and for boats to Djurgården and Nybroviken in the city (the latter run hourly — daily in summer and at weekends in winter; timetables can be found at www.ressel.se). So you could cut the walk short here if you wish to take the boat.

The main walk heads left here along Nackagatan to **Stock-holm's Transport Museum**. Admission is just 30kr, and the museum is much more than a collection of old trains and buses. It includes some amazing videos of Stockholm's street life in the 1960s and is worth the admission fee for these alone.

Carrying on beside the water, you soon reach **Danvikstulls Bridge**. Go under the bridge through the **tunnel** to the left. The path beyond here rises to **Fåfängan**. This hill, with a restaurant/café at the top, is another highlight offering more striking views — this time across the waters of **Saltsjön** plied by Helsinki-bound ferries. From here you can see right across to the city, Djurgården and out to the archipelago.

Modern apartments by the dockside at Hammarby Hamnen

Leaving Fåfängan, it is possible to walk back to Slussen via the ferry terminals (fairly short, but not very appealing). It is far preferable to retrace your steps back under Danvikstulls Bridge, then cross the bridge to **Henriksdal station**, from where you can catch the Saltsjöbanan train one stop to Slussen (if you are going to on Gondolen to eat;

see page 60). Or hop on one of the many buses to the same terminus.

Alternative walk: Årstaviken circuit. Follow the main walk to Nyfiken Gul café. Then, instead of walking under the bridges, turn left up the path that runs parallel with the large **indoor swimming pool**. At the top of this path, turn right on Ringvägen and after about 100m/yds, turn right at the **Ringen Shopping Centre**. This road quickly leads under a bridge, **Skanstullbron**. On the far side, follow the signs for 'Gullmarsplan'. This takes you to the left, under the railway, and then left again and up some stairs to **Gullmarsplan bus terminal**.

From the top of the stairs, turn left and walk with the entrance to the underground station on your left. After passing some shops and a square to your left, cross the road to the right, passing a video store and pizza restaurant on your left. Go over the pedestrian crossing and, straight away, descend the steps. Turn right and then immediately left along a path, heading steeply back down to the water's edge. After passing a boatyard, continue to skirt the water's edge. You are now walking in the opposite direction from where you came, on the other side of **Årstaviken**.

This side of the water is arguably the most beautiful — very tranquil, a waterside walk in the woods of **Årsta Forest**. It is lovely all year round, and the landscape and changes strikingly with the seasons. The path runs up to the two **railway bridges** and then crosses down into a former industrial area currently undergoing a lot of development as new waterside apartments are built. Keep to the path running between apartments and water, and stay with it as it dog-legs to the right and then left.

Following this route you come to another bridge, **Liljeholms-bron**. Climb the stairs up onto the bridge, then turn right and cross the bridge. Below you on the far side of the water you will see Café Loopen Marin (www.loopen.se) — a nice spot for a snack

View across Årstaviken to Årsta Forest

and glass of wine by the water in summer. Street (see page 86) is here, too, at the left-hand side of the bridge. At the end of the bridge you can either go straight on to Hornstull underground or turn right and follow Hornsgatan back to Zinkensdamm. But, more pleasantly, turn right and descend the path back into **Tantolunden**, stopping at Café Loopen Marin if you wish.

Otherwise, walk by the water for about 100m/yds, then take the first path to the left. Follow this in a straight line across the open park area, with the allotments and cottages of Tanto-lunden to your right. This leads to near where the walk began; you emerge on Ringvägen behind **Zinkensdamm Sports Stadium**, where you turn left to walk back to **Zinkensdamm underground station**.

Gondolen

Gondolen is not only a Stockholm institution, it's also a unique dining experience. Perched on a gantry with views over Lake Mälaren, the archipelago and the city, Gondolen offers a unique dining experience in an atmosphere that conjures up bygone days.

From Slussen, walk to the unmistakable structure and take the Katarina Hissen (Katarina Lift, costs 10kr) up to the gangway and restaurant. The lift dates back to 1883, when it was built to take people up to Mosebacke. The lift was completely rebuilt in 1935, and Gondolen opened its doors.

The main restaurant or outside terrace is the place to be if you want the view — make sure you book in advance!

GONDOLEN
Stadsgården 6, Stockholm (08 641 70 90. Open Mon-Fri 11.30-14.00 (lunch), 17.30-01.00, Sat 17.30-01.00; closed Sun. £££.

specialities include grilled char or halibut and fillet of prime veal

delicious **desserts** — don't miss the crème brûlée or warm cloudberries with vanilla ice cream

lunches at Gondolen are very good value for a venue in this price bracket; menus change weekly, with all starters for 95kr, mains for 185kr and desserts at 65kr, but above all the **dish of the day**, **weekly special**, **weekly vegetarian special** and **weekly salad** — all at 105kr

enormous range of **wines** and **champagnes** — from 72kr/ 255kr a bottle … up to 6,700kr a bottle from the specialist selection of French wines!

restaurants

eat

However, you can always have a drink at the bar and eat less expensively in the cosy, tiled 'kitchen' restaurant, which offers a simpler but still excellent menu; it has no views, but a charming atmosphere.

Gondolen, clockwise: the bar, outside terrace, a small part of the main dining area, the 'kitchen' restaurant

TWO WAYS WITH HERRING

Fried herring is a great standby dish for eating out on a budget —
it's often a main course in even the top restaurants, and at half the
price of the other dishes. Don't worry, no one will look down on
you for ordering it. Secondly, it's a cheap and easy dish that
anyone can prepare in a few minutes. Swedes swear that Baltic
herring, the smaller-sized relative of the North Sea herring, is best
for this dish.

Sill is raw marinated herring — a Swedish classic, often served
as a starter (as at Gondolen), where it is offered with cheddar
cheese and home-baked crisp bread. It also is an integral part of
most smorgasbords, again usually eaten first, before the hot
dishes. It can also be eaten on its own with boiled potatoes.

You'll see rack upon rack of *sill* for sale in the shops, usually in
glass jars and with a multitude of different flavourings. The
classics are *löksill* (with
onions) and *dillsill* (with dill),
but there are many other type
— like tomato, garlic and
even curry, to name but a few.

But it's easy to do your
own home-made *sill*. You can

Dillsill at Gondolen (above) and another attractive presentation (left)

either use salted herring fillets
or buy a ready-prepared 'base'
herring in a jar.

recipes

eat

Swedish *sill*

Soak the herring in cold water for 10 to 12 hours, or follow the directions on the package. Drain them.

Mix the sugar, vinegar and water in a bowl. Add the allspice, bay leaf and onion. Cut the herring in 1 cm thick slices (if not already sliced), cover with the dressing and refrigerate for at least two hours or overnight.

Serve garnished with red onion rings and dill sprigs.

Fried Baltic herring

Place the herring fillets skin side down. Salt and pepper them, then put the fillets together in pairs.

Roll the fillets in the flour and fry in butter until golden brown on both sides. Serve with mashed potatoes and lingonberries, as shown here.

Swedish sill

Ingredients (ample serving for 2 people)

4 to 6 fillets of salt herring or prepared base *sill*
150 ml sugar
100 ml Swedish spirit vinegar
200 ml water
5 tsp allspice
1 bay leaf
1 to 2 red onions
sliced dill sprigs

Fried Baltic herring

Ingredients (for 4-6 people)

1 kg Baltic herring fillet
2 red onions
Coarse rye flour
Salt
White pepper
Butter

Fried Baltic herring

An island of delights close to the city centre, Djurgården is a must-see on any trip to Stockholm. Whether you enjoy nature, history, wildlife, good food and drink or simply fine walking, Djurgården has it all. This introductory walk covers some of the major attractions, around which you can create variations to suit yourself.

djurgården and skansen

WALK

The suggested **starting point** is **Norrmalmstorg** (underground Östermalmstorg), so that you can ride on a vintage tram. Although this is privately run by volunteers (www.sparvagssallskapet.se), SL travelcards are valid on the line, which runs for 2.9km to Waldemarsudde, with several intermediate stops. It's a survivor from the much-mourned mass closure of the tram system in 1967 (but not, as sometimes incorrectly stated, the *only* survivor — there are two other original tram lines remaining, the Lidingöbanan and the Nockebybanan, although the latter has been totally modernised).

Distance: 4km/2.5mi — or more, depending on routes and attractions chosen. 1h30min minimum

Grade: easy; all paths are well-maintained year-round

Equipment: see pages 10-12; stout shoes, sun protection.

Transport: heritage 🚋 from Norrmalmstorg (trams run from Mar/Apr to Dec, about every 12min; journey time 5min). Or 🚌 47 from Centralen to various stops on Djurgården (every 10min; journey time 15min)

Refreshments en route: numerous cafés and restaurants

Points of interest:
Heritage tram
Nordic Museum
Vasa Museum
Rosendals Trädgård
Skansen
Gröna Lund
Numerous paths and trails around the island

You *could* take the tram to its terminus (there is even a rolling café on one of the trams, selling coffee, tea and a selection of cakes) but, for our suggested walk, alight at the third stop, for 'Nordiska museet/Vasamuseet', just after the tram crosses **Djurgårdsbron** onto the island of **Djurgården**.

To your right are two of the island's museums. Straight ahead of you is the **Nordic Museum** (Nordiskamuseet; www.

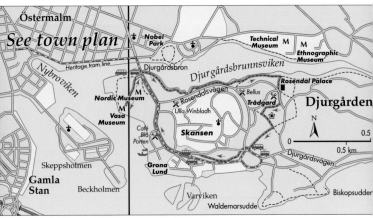

nordiskamuseet.se). Open daily, it is the largest collection of items relating to Swedish social history in the country. A short walk behind it is the much-celebrated **Vasa Museum** (Vasamuseet; www. vasamuseet.se). Also open daily (except major public holidays), it houses the warship Vasa, and is one of Sweden's most visited museums. The ship floundered and sank just a mile into her maiden voyage in 1628. Salvaged in 1961, the Vasa still requires ongoing work to prevent her wood from deteriorating and is preserved in a carefully-controlled environment.

Walk back to the **tram stop**, cross the road onto the side away from the Nordic Museum, retrace the tram line for around 30 metres/yards, and then turn right on a path by the water's edge. Go through the gates, following the sign for '**Djurgårds-terrassen**'. To the right is a grassy area, where many geese often congregate in summer. Follow the path by the water's edge for

Rosendals Trädgård: greenhouses selling organically grown plants; next door is the café described on page 70.

1.2km, until you come to **arrows** pointing to 'Boulehalllen/Rosendal/Trädgården/Terrassen' to the right. To your left is a jetty with seats.

Follow the path to the right up the slope. After about 150m/yds you reach **Rosendals Slott** (Palace) and its beautiful grounds. Walk straight ahead along Rosendalsvägen, with the grounds to your left. After another 100m you come to the grounds of Rosendals Trädgård on your right. The walkway goes straight through the centre of **Rosendals Trädgård** (rosendalstradgard.se), with the shops and café on your right and outdoor seating on the left.

At the end of the path, turn left and follow the path along the edge of the gardens. Keep along to a junction with another path, where you turn right. Stay on this path through the woods, and you come out on Djurgårdsvägen, with bus and tram stops. Turn right and follow the path up on the right, above the road. After another 500m/yds you come to the entrance to **Skansen** (see overleaf), with more bus and tram stops.

To complete the circuit, keep ahead and continue back to the tram stop at the museums. On your left it's impossible to miss the **Gröna Lund** funfair. Straight after this, Allmäna Gränd, on your left, leads to the **ferry terminal** if you want to catch the boat to Slussen. Just after crossing Allmäna Gränd is Café Blå Porten (see page 70).

SKANSEN

Skansen (www.skansen.se) is worth a day out itself. The world's oldest open-air museum and the largest in Sweden, it provides a unique picture of traditional life. Over 150 buildings from all over the country have been transported here and rebuilt piece by piece. Many of the buildings are open to the public, and staff in traditional dress give craft exhibitions.

There is also a zoo with a wide range of Nordic (and some non-Nordic) animals, where it is possible to see the normally reclusive lynx, bear and elk at close quarters. Skansen is also host to several activities, including the massively popular Swedish summer institution of Allsång på Skansen (sing-along at Skansen) and a Christmas market in December.

Skansen changes naturally with the seasons – in winter you can lose yourself in the stillness and feel

Ekshärad farmhouse (top), seal (right) and the Öland windmills

carried back in time; in summer it is a hive of activity, but so vast that you can always find a peaceful spot. Skansen is open daily (except Dec 24) from 10am; closing times vary.

Ulla Winbladh

There are well over a dozen places to eat and drink on Djurgården, from simple cafés to fine restaurants, so below and overleaf is just a small selection near the walk.

For more substantial fare, take a trip back in time at Ulla Winbladh. Food is served in an atmosphere that recalls bygone days, with the emphasis on Swedish tradition. The restaurant is named after a semi-fictional female libertine created by the Swedish poet and musician Carl Michael Bellman. The à la carte menu might cause a shock to the wallet, but there are fine Swedish staples at very affordable prices, including the lunch menu (11.30-14.30 Mon-Fri) — meatballs, Baltic herring à la Bellman, fish stew, and minced beef à la Ryder.

ULLA WINBLADH
Rosendalsvägen 8 (08 534 89 701
(www.ullawinbladh.se)
open daily from 11.30, from 12.00 at weekends £-£££

entrees like toast with shrimps, mayonnaise, dill and bleak roe; goose liver tureen with apple salad in lime dressing, with walnut bread

traditional fish dishes — such as fried Baltic herring with mashed potatoes and lingonberries; oven-baked Baltic herring with cream, anchovies, caviar and dill; fish casserole with vegetables, potatoes and shellfish sauce

meats — beef Rydberg: diced and fried fillet of beef sirloin served with fried potatoes and onions, egg yolk, Dijon mustard and Ulla Winbladh´s home-made mustard; meatballs with cream sauce, lingonberries and pickled cucumber

desserts — warm rosehip soup with vanilla ice cream and almond biscotti; cloudberry pudding with vanilla sauce; cinnamon doughnut with blueberry ice cream

restaurants

eat

Café Blå Porten (www.blaporten.com), Djurgårdsvägen 64, is a good choice in summer for tea or coffee and home-made cakes. It has a large inner courtyard and other nooks and crannies where you can find some peace and privacy. But on a windy autumn day, it's very cosy *inside*.

Rosendals Trädgård (www.rosendalstradgard.se), Rosendals-terrassen 12, is a garden specialising in the cultivation and sale of organic garden products. Here you can buy vegetables, herbs and plants, plus organic breads and other products. In addition, there

is a café which uses only organic products — including the drinks. It can be very popular at weekends, so try and visit out of peak times, when it has a much more relaxed atmosphere (it's open most

Café Blå Porten courtyard on a windy day in autumn (left) and Bellus (below)

days, but this varies according to the time of year, so check their web site).

Bellus, Sirishovsvägen 3, is another popular spot in the summer, with an appealing outdoor terrace and a Swedish-French menu with plenty of salads and grilled food.

CHANTERELLE MUSHROOM SOUP

It's barely an exaggeration to say that picking mushrooms is a national pastime in Sweden. The supply during the autumn is bountiful, and the chanterelle mushroom is king. But don't go mushroom-picking unless you know what you are doing or are with someone who does! Chanterelles are available these days in

the shops almost year-round; the price rockets out of season, but in September and October you'll find them in plentiful supply, reasonably priced.

Chop the onion very finely. Fry lightly in butter until just translucent. Cut the mushrooms into pieces, add to the onions and pour on the stock. Simmer for 10 min.

Blend the mixture thoroughly in a food processor, add the cream and mix with a wooden spoon. Simmer for a few minutes, then add the salt and pepper. Pour into bowls and sprinkle chopped parsley on top. Serve with a selection of dark Swedish soft bread and Swedish hard bread (see pages 78-79).

A warning for vegetarians: sadly, at present many soups in Sweden contain 'hidden' meat — chicken stock in mushroom soup or pork bits in pea soup. However, things are improving.

Ingredients (for 4 people)

400 g chanterelle mushrooms
1/2 large yellow onion or
   1 small yellow onion
400 ml vegetable stock
300 ml heavy cream
parsley for garnish
100 g butter (for frying and
   for bread)
pinch salt
1/2 tsp black or white pepper
Swedish soft and hard breads

recipes

eat

This easy, year-round walk is a Swedish classic and offers the visitor a real flavour of the outdoor life to be enjoyed in Stockholm — especially in summer. Sparkling water edged by forest, bathing beaches, sculptures dotted here and there — but most of all tranquillity and lovely views.

alvik

WALK

Alvik is the meeting point for three of Stockholm's railway systems: the underground 'green' line, tram line 12 (the Nockebybanan — a remnant from the once extensive tram network), and the Tvärbanan ('Crossways line'), a recent tram development with links to the southern and eastern sections of the underground.

Start out by leaving **Alvik station** via the terminus point for the **Tvärbanan**. From here you come out onto a modern square with the large **Salkhallen** tennis and sports centre. From here go left along Gustavslundsvägen, by the side of the hall. Follow this until you reach the waterside and Sjöpaviljongen restaurant (see page 77).

Distance: 5km/3mi; 1h45min

Grade: easy, with a few ascents and descents (50m/150ft overall). A few paths can be treacherous in winter.

Equipment: see pages 10–12; walking sticks; sun protection

Transport: U green line from Centralen to Alvik (journey time 13min, frequent service). Return via Nockebybanan 🚋 from Ålstens Gård to Alvik (journey time 9min, trams every 10-12min Mon-Sat, every 20min Sun), then change back to the green line to return to Centralen. *Note:* the Tvärbanan 🚋 from southern parts of Stockholm also serves Alvik (every 10-15min).

Refreshments: Restaurants Sjöpaviljongen and Himmel och Strand, both at the start of the walk

Points of interest
Waterside views
Sculptures
Solviksbadet
Alléparken

Just before the restaurant take the path to your right, beside the water, and cross a little **wooden bridge**. The path then follows a wooden walkway past Himmel och Strand (another restaurant described on page 77). Continue below the **bridge** carrying the Tvärbanan into Alvik and now enjoy good views

Watch for the unusual tennis-ball clock and outdoor thermometer on the roof of Salkhallen. Joining the waterside, you soon pass a striking sculpture of polished stainless steel — 'Havsvind', by Kent Ullberg.

across the short stretch of water to the island of Stora Essingen. One of the pleasures of this walk quickly becomes apparent — there are benches *everywhere*, certainly at almost every good vantage point.

The walk climbs some steps up to a junction: go left and follow the path downhill. This leads into the area known as **Äppleviken**, with a few houses and a small harbour. Pass these and then a rocky area by the water that is popular with bathers in summer. The waters of Lake Mälaren now open up to the left, and the walk enters one of its prettiest sections — strongly scented by pines.

Now you have to climb a bit — there are some railings to help, as it can be slippery here in winter. Coming to a fork, keep left, beside the water. You pass some houses and a minuscule beach, before having to take a short diversion by path and the road to round **Bergviks** boatyard and get back on the waterside path. There are many seats here, too, and

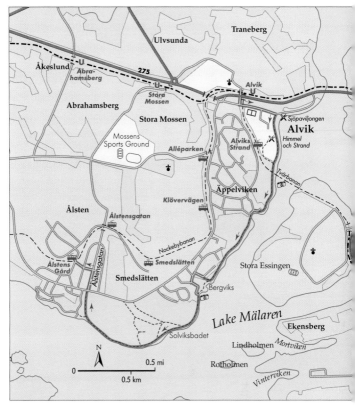

some gorgeous views out over the water, where many pleasure boats can be seen tootling along in summer.

A little further along you come to a 'classic' Swedish bathing centre, **Solviksbadet**. You step back into the Sweden of the 1970s — with mini-golf and ice cream stall. Past here, go up the hill to your left, still keeping towards the water; the path drops down again and follows a tranquil trail through trees before emerging at a park. Turn right now, away from the water, cross the **park**, and walk straight up Ålstensgatan. Take the first left, Gladbacken, which leads to the **tram stop at Ålstens Gård**. This is a residential area, but there is little bakery (open 10.00-18.00 Mon-Fri).

Take the Nockebybanan back to **Alvik**. The Nockebybanan was one of only two tram lines not closed in 1967 when Stockholm switched from left- to right-hand traffic. Before alighting at Alvik, perhaps first hop off for a few minutes at the penultimate stop, **Alléparken**, where the exteriors of the shops look little changed from the 1950s.

The idyllic setting of Restaurang Sjöpaviljongen at Alvik

This walk has two appealing restaurants shortly after the start of the walk (you could reverse the route if you want a meal to finish off the day). They share similar relaxing views over Lake Mälaren and have delightful outdoor areas open during summer. Weekday lunch is good value at both restaurants.

Restaurang Sjöpaviljongen *(shown left)*

Menus change with the seasons, but you can see the day's menu (or even book a table) on the web site — advance booking is recommended. There are cosy open fires in winter.

HIMMEL OCH STRAND *(shown below)*
Gustavslundsvägen 139, Alvik
(08 634 02 80 **open daily for lunch and most evenings (telephone ahead)** £-££

good-value **set lunch menus** Mon-Fri (usually one meat, one fish and one pasta dish)

strong **seafood theme** in the evenings

wine from only 165kr a bottle

RESTAURANG SJÖPAVILJONGEN
Tranebergs Strand 4, Alvik (08 704 04 24
www.sjopaviljongen.se (in English)
open 11.30-22.00 weekdays, 12.30-22.00 Sat, 12.30-21.00 Sun £££-£££

specialises in seafood — for example lemon sole or halibut, but also **meat** and **vegetarian** dishes

very popular **brunch buffet** at 195kr from 12.30-14.00 Sat, 12.30-17.00 Sun

---

Himmel och Strand

The evening menu, with an emphasis on seafood, features starters like smoked prawns with *aïoli* or three sorts of herring with Västerbotten cheese. The main courses are reasonably priced — try the grilled salmon with *wasabi aïoli,* spring onions and new potatoes.

restaurants

eat

SWEDISH BREADS

Traditional Swedish bread is generally wholesome and designed to be long-lasting. Many soft breads, such as *limpa,* are slightly sweetened with a small amount of syrup. Other soft breads range from simple white to really dark breads. Crisp bread *(knäckebröd, hårdbröd)* is a flat and dry bread or cracker. Its popularity stems from the fact that as long as it is stored in a dry place, it remains edible for a long time.

In restaurants, you'll almost always be offered a wide variety of breads — both soft and hard — with your meal. Try them all, to see which suits your taste!

Swedish crisp bread from Helsingland is the most common of the traditional Swedish hard breads — served as an accompaniment to a meal or, often, as a snack, topped with herring, cheese, or caviar from a tube and sliced egg. It is very good when made as a plain and simple crisp bread as in the recipe opposite — or you can spice it up with caraway, aniseed or fennel (or a mixture). The hole in the middle is for placing the bread on a stick.

Traditional Swedish breads being prepared at a food and drink festival in Stockholm

The recipe opposite comes from Lillemors Bak, a small independent bakery in Bollnäs in Helsingland, in the northeast of Sweden. Their web site (www.lillemorsbak.com) is only in Swedish, but has a lot of charming photographs.

Swedish crisp bread from Helsingland

Preheat the oven to 200°C, 400°F, gas mark 6.

Heat the milk and water so it is lukewarm, and dissolve the yeast in the liquid. Add the salt. Add the rye flour and stir in, and then add the wheat flour. Knead vigorously for at least five minutes.

Swedish hard (left) and soft flat breads and traditional baking tools. Note the hole in the middle of the hard bread.

Then divide the mixture into 20 parts and roll into balls. Let them rise, covered, for about 20 min. Using plenty of flour for rolling, roll out one piece at a time to a very thin circle, about 20 cm in diameter. Make a 2.5 cm hole in the middle and prick the surface all over with a fork.

Bake the breads one at a time on a dry tray in the oven for about 3-4 min. They should get nice and brown, but not too burnt.

Ideally, first place them on a net to cool and then store on a suitable stick — if you have one.

Ingredients (for 20 breads)

600 ml wheat flour
600 ml coarse rye flour
250 ml water
240 ml milk
50 g fresh yeast
2 tsp salt
flour for rolling out the breads

recipes

eat

This largely waterside walk runs from Bredäng to Liljeholm via Vinterviken; four very appealing cafés lie en route. Suitable for any time of the year, the walk is easily accessible, starting and ending at underground stations just a few minutes' ride from the city centre.

on the shores of lake mälaren

WALK

The walk begins at **Bredäng underground station**. There is only one exit, which leads out onto a square typical of Stockholm's suburbs. There's no reason to linger here, but there is a cash machine and shops where you can buy last-minute provisions.

From outside the station entrance turn left and pass the shops. Then take a path sloping down under a road bridge. Once under the road bridge, you come out into an open green area with some blocks of flats on the right. When you come to a fork, go right, following the yellow/ blue **'Hälsans Stig' sign** on a lamp-post.

Follow the path past a sign welcoming you to the Mälaren lakeside path ('Välkommen till BRF Mälarslingan') and continue between a group of houses for about 100m/yds, past a small car park on your

Distance: 7km/ 4.3mi; 2h30min

Grade: easy, with very few ascents, but some slight descents may be a bit tricky in winter. Good but sometimes stony paths. Easy to follow, with some 'Hälsans Stig' waymarking.

Equipment: see pages 10-12; walking sticks; sun protection.

Transport: U red line from T-Centralen or any other stop on the red line to Bredäng (journey time from T-Centralen 19min; trains every 10min). Return from Liljeholmen on the same underground route (journey time 10min).

Refreshments: Konditori Lyran (shortly after the start); midway along there are three cafés: Café Uddvillan (weekends only in winter), Vinter-viken, and Kafé Pladder (only open late spring to autumn)

Points of interest:
Lake Mälaren
Swedish villas
Vinterviken's gardens and sculptures
Lake Trekanten

Short walks: Start or end the walk at Aspudden underground station, a 10-minute walk from Vinterviken. Walk to/from Vinterviken or to/from Bredäng or Liljeholmen (all versions about 3km/ 2mi).

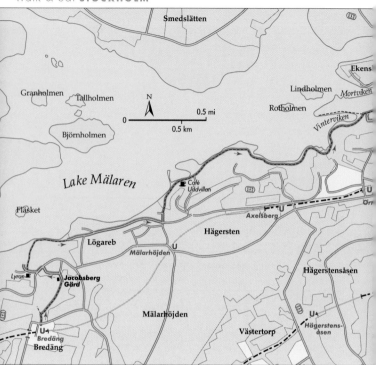

right and **Jakobsbergs Gård**, a mansion dating from the 18th century (not open to the public). Carry on by turning left along 'Oddfellowsstigen', past some more houses, until you come to a T-junction, from where the water of **Lake Mälaren** can be glimpsed through the trees ahead.

Cross the road (Algrytevägen) and follow it to the left down-hill for about 50m/yds, to the sign for Konditori Lyran (nor-

Jakobsbergs Gård

mally open from 11am (closing times vary; see www.konditorilyran.se — the opening times on the home page, in Swedish, are just about decipherable). If you're not visiting Lyran, there is a path just before the café with a 'Hälsans Stig' sign that goes down to the water. Alternatively there are some wooden steps behind the café.

Coming down to the path below Lyran, there is an area to the left with seats looking out across the water — perfect for picnics or a coffee stop. Otherwise turn right and take the path through the woods. After about 50m/yds, the path swings to

Lyran (top) and the herb garden at Kafé Pladder

the left and over a **waterfall**. A short way further along, the path merges with a road marked 'Pettersbergsvägen'. You are now in a unique area of Stockholm, with many **different styles of villa** perched on the hillside. This is one of the few areas in Stockholm that still has wooden telegraph poles, and it has an almost Mediterranean feel.

After walking along the road for about 15 minutes, you come to a **small square with a water trough**. Turn left down Källbacken, walk between two houses and emerge in an open grassy area with **Lake Mälaren** to your left. After about 150m/yds the path skirts a **boatyard**, on the far side of which is Café Uddvillan (open weekends 11.00-17.00, open on weekdays in summer). They serve coffee, home-baked bread and, during summer, lunches. In addition to a beautiful view of Lake Mälaren, this café has regular art exhibitions.

From here the path continues past some allotments and through woods. After about 100m/yds you will come to two grey stones where the path narrows as it turns left to meander pleasantly beside the water and swing round past another

boatyard. Past here, with some flats to your right, keep by the water, following the sign for '**Vinterviken**' along a wooden platform by the water's edge. Once round a bend, the way is again a path which widens as you approach Vinterviken.

To your left is a large former factory, now housing a café (particularly popular with young families), but from spring to autumn a better bet is to continue *past* this building for about five more minutes, with allotments to your right. This brings you to Kafé Pladder, an open-air café amongst **herb gardens and sculptures**. The café serves a wide range of food and drink and has some lovely hidden corners, ideal for relaxing with a book (though it gets extremely busy on weekend afternoons).

Beyond Kafé Pladder the path runs under a large road bridge and past a couple of villas before coming to a road with **Lake Trekanten** in front of you. You can walk along either side of this lake, but the path to the right is more pleasant. In winter people sometimes walk straight across the ice (but this can be exceedingly dangerous; see under 'Winter' on page 8).

At the far side of the lake **Liljeholmen underground station** is just ahead. You can return into town from here or just go one stop on the underground to Hornstull (or walk*), where there are several restaurants and cafés (including Street; see overleaf).

*To walk on to Hornstull, head left, past the underground station. At the top of a rise you come out on Liljeholmsvägen (with tram tracks). Cross this road and go right, alongside the tram lines, for about 30m/yds, then take the steps to the overpass. At the top, take the road to the left and keep straight on, crossing the road bridge (**Liljeholmsbron**) into **Hornstull** (see map on pages 54-55).

Street

Street is just a short hop from the end of this walk, at Hornstull. Walk over Liljeholmsbron and it's just to your left, below the bridge, at the waterside. Street is the success story that they said

could never happen in Sweden — Stockholm's first permanent art, music and design market inspired by Spitalfields in London.

Received wisdom dictated that there would be too many obstacles, that the strict Swedish laws governing business, food and drink — to say nothing of the harsh winters, would make it impossible for the idea to flourish. Street's driving force, John Higson, defied the cynics, and the whole project is going from strength to strength. It has quickly grown from a few outdoor stalls to an indoor and outdoor centre for markets, music, art, performance, food and drink. Moreover, it's become an integral part of the Hornstull community.

STREET
Hornstulls Strand 9, Stockholm
www.streetinstockholm.se (08 658
63 50. Open Sun-Tue 10.00-17.00,
Wed-Sat 10.00-midnight £-££

serves **food produced by local farmers** (most of the suppliers are members of a web-based network called 'Farmers Own').

good value lunches on weekdays (served from 11.30-14.00) — a different meat, fish, vegetarian, soup or salad dish every day (mains 89kr, soups 65kr, salads 78kr)

wide-ranging **evening menu** that changes with the seasons

restaurants
eat

SWEDISH PANCAKES

Pancakes are eaten all year round in Sweden. They are a traditional Thursday lunch dessert, eaten with lingonberry jam (as shown here) and/or thick whipped cream. Lingonberries are a staple in Swedish cuisine and can be found as jams in all supermarkets. They grow plentifully in the forests but are fairly tart, hence their common use as jam.

Whisk the eggs, add the milk, flour and salt and beat until smooth. Medium heat a large frying pan with a small amount of butter. For each pancake, pour about 1/4 to 1/2 cup batter into the pan (depending on its size): the bottom of the pan should be covered but the pancakes should be very thin.

Cook for about 2 min, turn with a spatula and cook for about another minute, until golden brown. Serve warm, sprinkled with sugar if desired. Top with *Drottning sylt,* a delicious jam made of blueberries and raspberries (available from most supermarkets). You can also serve with fresh berries and/or cream according to taste. The latter is the traditional Swedish way of serving, but of course a whole range of other toppings can be used, for example vanilla ice cream or maple syrup.

Ingredients (for 4 people)
3 free range/organic eggs
1-1/4 cups flour
2-1/2 cups full fat milk
1/2 tsp salt
butter
1 jar *Drottning sylt* (jam)
whipped cream
sprinkling sugar
other optional toppings/fillings

recipes

eat

Drottningholm, the official residence of the Swedish royal family on the island of Lovön, is a worthwhile day trip in itself. But its chief attraction is the extensive gardens which provide great walking year round — as well as walks beyond the palace, including a specially-designed nature trail.

drottningholm palace and lovön
WALK

Starting from **Nockeby**, take the steps out of the **tram station** and join Nockeby Kyrkvägen. Walk towards the striking **Sankta Birgitta Church**, built in 1962. Just before the church take the path to the right that leads to the steps and a footbridge. *Don't* cross the footbridge, but take the steps down to the main road and turn left. You can either take the 1km/0.6mi walk along Drottningholms-vägen (including a swing-bridge), or take bus 176/177 or 323 for the short ride to Drottningholm.

After crossing the **swing-bridge**, the small island of **Kärsön**, and a second, smaller **bridge**, you come to the road leading into Drottningholm. Here, on the left, is the departure/arrivals **quay for the boats from Stadshuset**. Follow the boulevard until you reach **Drottningholm**

Distance: 6.5km/4mi; 2h30min

Grade: easy, mainly on well-maintained, signposted footpaths

Equipment: see pages 10-12; walking sticks; sun protection

Transport: It's most interesting to go by tram one way and boat the other. The most common tourist route is by 🚢 Strömma Kanalbolaget steam-boat from Stadshuset (City Hall), which takes a short cruise on Lake Mälaren to the entrance to the castle (www.strommakanalbolaget.se; 130kr one way). We recommend this for the *return*. The boats run between May 1 and the end of Oct (hourly and half-hourly until mid-Sep, then twice-daily at weekends from mid-Sep until the end of Oct). To get to Drottningholm by tram, take either the **U** green line underground or the 🚊 Tvärbanan light railway to Alvik, then change to 🚋 tram to Nockeby. The Nockeby-banan tram is part of the Stockholms-lokaltrafik network (see pages 14-15).

Refreshments: café near the castle entrance and Chinese Pavilion kitchen offering light refreshments; full meals and light refreshments on board boats to Drottningholm

Points of interest:
Drottningholm Palace and grounds
Drottningholm nature trail *(naturstig)*

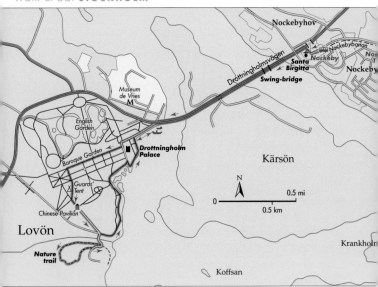

Palace, a UNESCO World Heritage Site (www.royalcourt.se). Turn left here to visit the palace; otherwise walk straight on, to come to the **Baroque Garden**. Created in the 17th century, it features over 300 lime trees. Take your time and enjoy its spectacular avenues, as well as the large park known as the **English Garden** which stretches away to your right.

As you walk down the avenue you will pass the **water parterre** and then a **fountain**. After the fountain, take the next turning to the left. Follow this path past the unusual **guards' tent** — like the one on page 26, but this one built of wood — and after this the **Chinese pavilion** (paid admission), built in 1753.

Take the route directly behind the Chinese pavilion, a tree-lined avenue which leads to the palace's nature trail *(naturstig)*. The path follows a short trail through the woods, with information en route about the cultural history, nature and animals on **Lovön Island**, where Drottningholm is located. Unfortunately the information panels are only in Swedish.

The guards' tent at Drottningholm dates back to 1781: unlike the ones at Haga Park, this is built of wood. It housed the dragoons of King Gustav III.

After your visit, return to the **quayside** for the **steamboat back to Stadshuset** — perhaps with a slap-up meal on board!

Some unusual objects are seen on the trail, like this automatic feeder for wild animals. On most trails you will find fallen trees near or across the paths; trees are left to die at their own pace in Sweden, and the trunks left to decay naturally.

SAIL AND EAT

Strömma Kanalbolaget run a variety of cruise options to Drottningholm where you can combine a meal on board with a visit to the palace and grounds.

If you want to go for 'the works', you can take an evening cruise in the summer (Tue-Thu from late June to late August). This combines a boat trip there and back, a three course meal, and a guided tour of the park for 450kr. There is also a round-trip lunch package for 310kr or an dinner cruise where you choose from the à la carte menu.

TYPICAL MENU

starters: archipelago tartar on toast with salmon, prawns & mustard or air-dried ham with asparagus, rocket, sliced parmesan, olive oil & croutons

main courses: seared fillet of char with root vegetables julienne and soft whey cheese sauce or roast fillet of beef with bacon, mushrooms, onions, spring vegetables and Madeira sauce

desserts: fresh fruit salad with vanilla ice cream and wafer or cloudberry parfait with sugar-stirred raspberries and wafer

Västerbotten cheese quiche
<u>Ingredients (for 4 portions)</u>
<u>for the pie case</u>
125 g butter
300 ml flour

<u>for the filling</u>
225 g grated Västerbotten cheese
  (Västerbottensost)
100 ml milk or cream
3 organic eggs
salt and pepper

restaurants

eat

VÄSTERBOTTEN CHEESE QUICHE

The key ingredient for this pie is the strong cheese named after the Västerbotten region in the north of Sweden. It's a hard cow's milk cheese with small holes. As with cheddar, the curd is heated, cut, and stirred before the cheese is moulded and aged for 12-14 months. Salty and bitter, it is considered by some to be Sweden's best cheese; demand has often outstripped the limited supply.

This recipe is from Simons Skafferi (see also page 32). See ingredients opposite.

Cut the (fridge)-cold butter into cubes and mix with the flour. Add the water and then the lemon rind and work the mixture through the fingers. Let the mixture rest for 30 min, then press it out into a pie dish (24cm in diameter). Bake the crust in the oven at 220°C, 425°F, gas mark 7 for 15 min. Take out the crust and lower the oven to 200°C, 400°F, gas mark 6.

Whisk the eggs so they have light bubbles, then add the cream. Add the grated cheese, salt and pepper. Fill the pie crust, put it back in the oven and cook for 25 min until golden brown. Serve with vegetables or a mixed salad.

Västerbotten cheese was reputedly invented in the village of Burträsk in the 1870s, supposedly by a dairy maid, Eleonora Lindström. Legend has it that she was stirring the curd of a traditional cheese and was interrupted — by other jobs (or, in a more racey tale, by her lover). This resulted in alternating periods of heating and stirring the mixture.

recipes

eat

This excursion, combining two heritage railways and a steamboat trip on Lake Mälaren, makes for a great day out, with a visit to two castles set in lovely grounds and with plenty to see and do — Gripsholm and Taxinge. The trip outlined in the panel is only possible *on weekends in summer*, but there are many other options.

gripsholm and taxinge castles

EXCURSION

While the logistics panel at the right gives one option (so that you can travel on *both* heritage railways and the steamboat), this excursion has a multitude of possible permutations — depending on how much or how little you want to pack into a day.

Round-trip tickets including the steamboat, narrow-gauge steam railway and then regular train back to Stockholm are available for 250kr. These are sold on board the steamship and at the Sverige-huset tourist information centre (see page 20).

The **steamboat S/S Marie-fred** (www.mariefred.info) has a remarkable history; she has been plying the waters of Lake Mälaren since 1903. On board you can enjoy snacks or a full meal (with steak and salmon among the dishes on offer). S/S Mariefred sails from Klara Mälarstrand, next to Stockholm's City Hall, on Saturdays and Sundays from late May until early September, and Tuesdays to Sundays between mid-June and mid-August. The boat departs Stockholm at 10.00, taking three and a half hours, and returns from Mariefred at 16.30. *But on weekends from May to*

Departures: 🚂 from Centralen to Läggesta, 70km southwest of central Stockholm (10.55 daily; journey time 39min). Change to the narrow-gauge Östra Södermanlands Järnväg 🚂 and take it to Mariefred. After visiting Gripsholms Slott, take the ⛴ S/S Mariefred to Taxinge-Näsby. Return to Läggesta Nedre with the standard-gauge 🚂 1950s railcar, then regular 🚂 back to Centralen. *This is only one travel option — see text for more.*

Refreshments: cafés in Mariefred and at Taxinge Slott

Points of interest:
Östra Södermanlands Järnväg narrow-gauge railway
Gripsholms Slott
'olde worlde' Mariefred
steamboat trip
Taxinge Slott

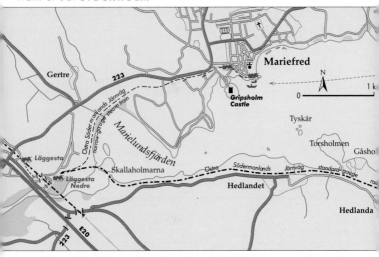

September she makes the short 25-minute connecting **trip between Mariefred and Taxinge-Näsby** and back, leaving Mariefred at 13.50 and returning from Taxinge-Näsby at 15.55.

The other veteran mode of transport to both Gripsholms Slott/Mariefred and Taxinge Slott is the **heritage railway, Östra Södermanlands Järnväg** (www.oslj.nu). They run **two lines — a narrow-gauge steam railway to Mariefred and a 1950s railcar on a standard-gauge line to Taxinge-Näsby**. Both train lines run on weekends from the beginning of May till the end of September and daily from late June until about mid-August.

To get to the steam train, take the regular train (www.sj.se) from Centralen to **Läggesta**. On alighting, walk from the back of the train down the full length of the platform, following **signs for the 'steam railway'**. At the end of the platform, you will see

over the line and rebuilt it as a narrow (600mm/2ft)-gauge line. It has grown over the years and now has an extensive museum of locomotives, including steam and even battery-powered engines. Most trains run the full 4km/ 2.5mi from Läggesta to

Östra Södermanlands Järnväg operates a narrow-gauge steam railway to/from Mariefred and a 1950s diesel railcar on a standard-gauge line to/from Taxinge-Näsby.

the tracks and buildings of Östra Södermanlands Järnväg below you, reached by a sloping dirt path. The timetable on their web site shows which trains run in connection with arrivals from Stockholm. This line from Läggesta to Mariefred was originally the state-run standard-gauge line, but it closed in the 1960s. The Östra Södermanlands Järnväg Society from nearby Södertälje subsequently took

Taxinge Slott (top; web site and opening times opposite) and Gripsholms Slott (www.gripsholmsslott.se; open daily from mid-May to mid-Sep from 10.00-16.00; admission 70kr) — both castles are set in beautiful grounds by the waters of Lake Mälaren.

Mariefred (with intermediate stops along the way), while a few travel down to the docks to meet the incoming/outgoing steamboat. Tickets are available from 50kr upwards, and there is both third and second class accommodation — the latter with softer seats!

The **line between Läggesta Nedre and Taxinge-Näsby** was reopened in 1998 after the state-run line closed in 1995. It is a single track, 7km/4.3mi long, with just one form of motive power — a 1950s railcar which runs five times a day in each direction. *Note:* You can also get to Taxinge with an SL card: take the local train from Centralen to Södertälje and change there to a 780 bus, then alight at Värsta Backe for bus 782 to Taxinge (total journey time about 1h45min). The 782 runs a limited service, so check details before departing.

However you travel, the small village of **Mariefred** is worth a stroll, with some old-fashioned craft stores, but the highlights of the trip are the two castles and their surroundings. Gripsholm Castle belongs to the Swedish Royal Family.

Taxinge Slott

This castle (www.taxingeslott.se; see photograph opposite) is about a 10-minute walk from Taxinge-Näsby station. Note that the castle often hosts auctions, wedding receptions and other events — when it can be very crowded, so it is worth telephoning to enquire in advance. The castle's history is interesting — see the (English) web page.

Taxinge Krog

On the walk between Taxinge station and the castle, you pass Taxinge Krog — the closest you will get to a genuine Swedish country pub.

TAXINGE SLOTT
at Taxinge Slott, (0159 70114 £-££
castle and café open 11.00-16.00/18.00
most weekends year round and daily from
May-Sep

the café does sandwiches and the like, but is famous for its **cake buffet** (shown above), with around 60 different types of locally baked cakes!

full restaurant service only for events

TAXINGE KROG
Näsby Handel, Nykvarn, (0159 70017
(www.taxingekrog.se – only in Swedish, but
very tempting photos) ££
open Sat/Sun from 12.00-21.00 in Apr/May,
Tue-Sun from 12.00-22.00 from Jun to mid-
Aug, Sat/ Sun from 12.00-22.00 from mid-
Aug to mid-Sep. Open daily from late Nov
until just before Christmas to serve a
Christmas smorgasbord, Mon-Fri from
12.00-18.00, Sat/Sun from 13.00-18.00
(425 kr excluding drinks).

summer menu offers three courses at quite reasonable prices; **children's menus** also available

restaurants

eat

No trip to Stockholm is complete without sampling the Stockholm archipelago. With around 24,000 islands, the choice is wide, but Grinda is ideal for a day trip or short stay. The island is easy to get to, beautiful, has cottage accommodation and a renowned restaurant.

grinda

EXCURSION

2

The Stockholm archipelago is worthy of a holiday in itself – many visitors spend weeks island-hopping, while others retreat to one of its many residences — from simple cottages to grand villas — for the whole summer. But for just a taste of the islands, Grinda is ideal. It's a long enough journey to get a real feel of the archipelago and, once there, the island offers a plenty of choice, with cottages for hire, a high-quality restaurant, a shop and — above all, peace and quiet.

Whichever boat you take, it will sail through the inner archipelago, past **Djurgården** and **Lidingö** on the left, and then out through the network of islands, stopping to pick up and drop off passengers at several little docks. The boat also calls at the spa town of **Vaxholm**, a popular tourist spot, before heading on to

Departures: 🚢 daily from Strömkajen (outside the Grand Hotel) and Strandvägen; sailing time 1h20min to 2h30min (operator Waxholmsbolaget (www.waxholmsbolaget.se). It is also possible to take 🚌 437 from Slussen to Lillsved (journey time 50min) and then Waxholmsbolaget 🚢 steamboat to Grinda (sailing time 10min).

Refreshments: on board or at Grinda Wärdshus (see page 104).

Hints: The options for boat travel to Grinda are many and varied. The vastly complex timetables (available from outside Waxholmsbolaget's offices at Strömkajen) are only in Swedish, so ask at the offices if you need help planning your trip. There are many departures in summer; in winter only a skeleton service is run, and it can be difficult to get there and back in one day. The fastest, but less charming option is to take a modern 'Cinderella' boat from Strandvägen; the ideal option is steamboat (daily from Jun to mid-Aug, weekends only from mid-May to mid-Sep). Travel just as passengers did a century ago, and treat yourself to a meal on board (see page 105), with prices to suit every budget. The boat takes you through the inner archipelago, with great views of the islands along the way.

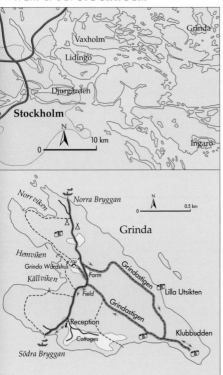

Grindastigen

This waymarked 2.5km/ 1.6mi walk is easy, but stout walking boots are recommended, as it can be muddy or waterlogged in places. The walk is an easy-to-follow, almost cir-cular route.

Just past the farm, follow the 'Grindastigen' sign to the right, taking the path into the woods. Then just keep to the main path — perhaps branching off to 'Lilla Utsikten' and 'Klub-budden', for good views over the water (ideal picnic spots).

The path heads southeast and then swings back round until it comes to the back of the fields with sheep and cows. The easiest route back is to follow the path with the edge of the field on your right, crossing the wooden animal grill and the field, to come out at the junction where you can take the path to Grinda Wärdshus.

Grinda. Some boats stop at Södra (south) Grinda, others at Norra (north) Grinda; the south stop is more convenient.

Assuming you arrive at **Södra Grinda**, alight from the boat and

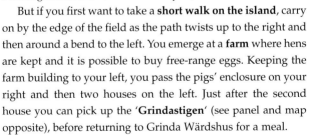

Sign on the Grindastigen, indicating the way to the cottages. Grinda's forest is remarkable for its deep, dark green early autumn colours. The simple island cottages are run by the Grinda Wärdshus.

follow the main path up the hill. Shortly you come to a building marked 'Expedition' — the **reception** if you are staying in a cottage and also good for maps, etc. Carrying straight on past this office, there is a field on the right of the path where the island's sheep and cows graze. Beyond the field, you come to a fork: to the left is the short path to Grinda Wärdshus with its indoor and summer outdoor restaurants (you can see the main building across the field in front of you).

But if you first want to take a **short walk on the island**, carry on by the edge of the field as the path twists up to the right and then around a bend to the left. You emerge at a **farm** where hens are kept and it is possible to buy free-range eggs. Keeping the farm building to your left, you pass the pigs' enclosure on your right and then two houses on the left. Just after the second house you can pick up the '**Grindastigen**' (see panel and map opposite), before returning to Grinda Wärdshus for a meal.

Grinda Wärdshus

If you want to stop overnight, Grinda Wärdshus is not only a famous restaurant, but a hotel, also offering cottage and hostel accommodation. For a taste of archipelago accommodation Swedish style, the summer cottages are recommended. They have mains electricity, beds, cooker, fridge and plentiful crockery and

cutlery. You will need to bring your own sheets (or sleeping bag) and pillowcases … *and* any alcoholic beverages you may need — there's no state-run Systembolaget 'alcohol shop' on the island. A torch is essential, and it's a good idea to bring your own food (there is a shop, but it's pricey and closed in low season). 'Eco toilets' and showers are located a short walk away from the cottages.

GRINDA WÄRDSHUS
Grinda. (08 542 49 491; www.grindawardshus.se **££-£££**

menus vary seasonally; the **emphasis is on locally-sourced foods**

specialities include fish and shellfish casserole with garlic mayonnaise and croutons; corn-fed chicken from the island of Öland, served with rice-style pasta, roasted bell peppers, rosemary and parsley; sautéed salmon from Vanö with potatoes and anchovy, shrimp and horseradish sauce; feta cheese from Ljusterö with couscous, roasted summer vegetables and tomato concasse; farm-raised cod with chorizo sausage, sautéed vegetables, creamed potatoes with olives and red wine sauce

elaborate sweets — like a combination of cappuccino, Bailey's and chocolate truffle, or violet panna cotta with spice-marinated blackberries

---

restaurants
eat

Veteran steamboats

Waxholmsbolaget has two veteran steamboats, Norrskär, built in 1910, and Storskär, built in 1908 and therefore celebrating its 100th birthday. Both boats have quite brilliant design features to maximise one's enjoyment of the archipelago. Outdoor seating is carefully sheltered at the boat's aft, with latticed railings and windows designed to give maximum all-round visibility. Indoors there are lounges plus the boats' celebrated dining rooms.

The S/S Storskär — 100 years old

A **meal on board** is recom-mended and does not have to break the bank. You can dine during one of the regular trips or by taking an all-day or evening round-trip cruise. For tour information see the Waxholmsbolaget web site (www.waxholmsbolaget.se; in English) or telephone 08 679 58 30 (to book a table call 08 24 30 90). The trips are *very* popular, but if you are able to travel out of the high season there is a lot more room to move about the boats!

The restaurants are quite reasonably priced, with main meals starting as low as 100kr for traditional fried herring and potatoes. If you just want to snack or are on a tight budget, the boats also have very reasonably priced cafeterias offering good traditional food from just 45kr (like herring on crispbread), and wine at just 40kr a glass — very reasonable for Swedish wine prices!

Fjäderholmarna, the Feather Islands, make for an ideal day trip for those who want a taste of the Stockholm archipelago without taking a long boat journey. The main island, while only half a kilometre broad at its widest point, is home to restaurants, cafés, shops, museums and many secluded spots.

fjäderholmarna

EXCURSION

If you catch the **boat from Nybroplan**, you will sail past the grand buildings of **Strandvägen** to your left and then through the channel between **Skeppsholmen** on your right and **Djurgården** on your left. Looking to your left, you pass the Gröna Lund funfair before emerging into **Saltsjön**, the start of the main route through the archipelago, where you will almost certainly see one or more of the passenger ferries for Finland and Estonia moored on your right. The boat then sails past the residential areas of **Henriksdal** and **Nacka** up on the hills to your right (with Djurgården still on your left). At the end of this channel, the boat may make a short stop at **Nacka Strand** to pick up/ drop off passengers before the short hop to **Stora Fjäderholmen**.

The **boat trip from Slussen** is the same, except that it

Departures: Two lines serve Fjäderholmarna (sailing time 25min each way). Stromma Kanalbolaget run boats from Nybroplan (a short walk from Östermalmstorg **U** underground station or 47, 69, 76). Daily from late Apr till early Sep (hourly from 10.00-23.30, half-hourly from mid-May to mid-Aug). Fjäderholmslinjen boats sail from Slussen (a short walk from Slussen **U** underground station or 2, 43, 55). Daily from late Apr to early Sep (hourly from 10.00 till midnight). Both lines charge 90kr for the return trip.

Refreshments: many cafés and restaurants on Fjäderholmarna

Hints: Stromma Kanalbolaget use modern, spacious tourist boats, while Fjäderholmslinjen run a ferry built in the late 19th century. This excursion is very popular with day-trippers, and the boats can get very busy in peak season and on weekends — often with standing room only on the boats from Slussen. However, if you wait until mid- to late afternoon there is usually much more room — well worth it, to avoid stress and to take in the views from on board. Outside late Apr to early Sep, service to the Fjäderholmarna (operated by Waxholmsbolaget) is very limited, and all the facilities are closed.

begins at Slussen, with **Gamla Stan** receding behind you and
the ferry terminals to your left, before taking the same route as
described above.

The boats dock in front of an **information office**. Here you
can pick up leaflets about this main island in English. For much
of the 20th century Stora Fjäderholmen was used by the
Swedish Navy and thus a prohibited area until 1985. Later the
island was developed as a tourist destination.

Leaving the boat, turn right and walk past the small **marina**
and follow the path which skirts close to the island's shores. In
summer, all the best vantage points beside the water are quickly
taken up by sunbathers and picnickers. The path swings round

to the left, and before you
reach the group of buildings
there is a path up to your left
marked '**Trädgården**'. Don't
miss this! Here you can find
light snacks, coffee, biscuits
and soft drinks, all at very low
prices. You can rent a blanket,
family games, play *boules* — even
pick your own rhubarb and
raspberries when they are in
season. In addition, you can bring
your own picnic and eat at the
tables provided or on the grass.

When you can tear yourself
away from the garden, there is

more to see. Go back down the path from where you entered the garden, turn left, and by the water you will see Fjäderholmarnas Magasin, a café/restaurant offering lunches, seafood or grill buffet and picnic hampers. Next to Fjäderholmarnas Magasin is a row of shops selling local handicrafts, while on the main path is **Verkstadlängan** (Workshop Row), with shops selling home-crafted glasswork, woodwork and so on.

Flower-decked shop and below, one of the secluded corners where you can get away from the crowds

Continue along the main path to another **marina**, just in front of which is an exhibition of traditional boats and charcoal drawings by Harald Lindberg, whose works evoke the life of people in the archipelago in the first half of the last century. This is a pleasant place to linger, amid the distinctive 'smoky' smell of the old boats.

Passing the marina and almost coming full circle, to your right is the restaurant Fjäderholmarnas Krog and, continuing round to our starting point, the Smokery Restaurant (Rökeriet). The area around here can get very congested in the afternoons during high season as people get on and off the boats.

Fjäderholmarnas Krog and Rokeriet

Fjäderholmarnas Krog is the more 'upmarket' of these two restaurants, both of which serve traditional seafood and meat dishes. The food is good, but all on the pricey side — over 300kr for many main courses, and a glass of wine for no less than 80kr!

FJÄDERHOLMARNAS KROG
Stora Fjäderholmen (08 718 33 55
Open from lunch until late evening,
daily, late Apr to mid-Sep £££

eight **entrees** — like herring, salads, lobster, gazpacho

five kinds of **fish**, including fish soup and seafood platter

meat: beef, lamb, entrecote

seasonal **vegetarian dish**

several **desserts**, such as crème brûlée, strawberries, chocolate tart

Fjäderholmarnas Krog — idyllic, but very pricey. Nearby Rokeriet has some more affordable dishes in its café section.

ROKERIET
Stora Fjäderholmen (08 716 50 88
Open from lunch until late evening,
daily, late Apr to mid-Sep ££

seafood buffet a speciality

also **à la carte menu** and **light meals/snacks** from the café

restaurants

eat

SURSTRÖMMING

Surströmming is the Swedish dish that arouses the greatest passions — love or hate, with little in between. It's fermented Baltic herring, found in supermarkets from around mid-August until late autumn. The herring are caught in spring, fermented in barrels and then tinned, where they continue to ferment. By the early autumn, gases produced by bacteria have built up … making the tins bulge. Don't worry — they won't explode!

Nevertheless, opening the tins is a unique experience, and *must be done outdoors*, preferably well away from any homes (not on an apartment balcony!). A powerful rotten-egg odour is released, and there is a skill in not letting the noxious brine spurt out onto one's clothes! One option to reduce the smell is to open the can under water. Because of its strong flavour, you only need a little bit!

Butter the bread and top it with some onion and potato (which can be used hot or cold). Now comes the tricky part. Take a whole fish from the tin, using a fork, slice it down the middle and remove the insides. Use the fork to stamp the fish to loosen the bones and then fillet it. Add some fish pieces to the bread, fold, and eat as a sandwich. Some people also like to add a dollop of crème fraîche.

Salty *surströmming* is thirst-inducing. Traditionally it was drunk with milk or shots of spirit like *aquavit*. But almost any drink is suitable — from beer to *must* or *svagdricka* (see pages 40-41).

Ingredients (for 4 portions)
tinned *surströmming*
tunnbröd (thin, soft bread sold in sheets)
red onion, sliced or diced
mandelpotatis (almond potatoes), boiled and peeled
butter

recipes

eat

Easily accessed using the charming Saltsjöbanan light railway, this walk takes in a beach/bathing area, a small nature reserve by a lovely lake, and the spa terminus of Saltsjöbaden — to say nothing of four very appealing cafés.

erstaviksbadet and saltsjöbaden

WALK

Alighting at **Östervik**, leave the station and turn right along a small road. Follow the road, keeping right; beyond a post box you join a main road. Continue up the main road, parallel with the railway line to your right, for about five minutes, until you come to a 30km/h speed limit sign and a junction to the left, with a **wooden sign** marked 'Erstavik'. Turn left on this road, walking under a **motorway** and past a **stable**. Very little traffic uses this road, and it is a pleasant walk through open fields where horses from the stable graze.

After about 10 minutes the surroundings become more wooded; keep to the road for about 3.5km/2.2mi, until you reach an area with more mixed woodland and pasture, and a few summer cottages. Keeping to the road and ignoring a fork downhill to

Distance: 7.5km/4.7mi; 2h45min

Grade: easy; very few ascents or descents. Good, but sometimes stony paths, some of which may be slippery or waterlogged in winter. Easy to follow, with several signposts.

Equipment: see pages 10-12; walking sticks; sun protection.

Transport: Saltsjöbanan light 🚆 from Slussen to Östervik (journey time 15min), Erstaviksbadet (journey time 25min; change trains at Igelboda), or Saltsjöbaden (journey time 26min). Trains run every 20min (every 30min in summer and at off-peak times); SL passes and other discount tickets are valid. NB: the Saltsjöbanan may close for a major renovation in 2009.

Refreshments: Erstaviksbadet kiosk/café mid-way through the walk (weekdays in summer, up to late Sep if the weather is good); Bistro Solsidan (Solsidan station, good lunch deals), Stationshuset café (Saltsjöbaden station), Café Bryggan (Saltsjöbaden)

Points of interest:
Saltsjöbanan light railway
Erstaviksbadet and nature reserve
Saltsjöbaden

Short walk: Start or end the walk at Erstaviksbadet station, walking from or to Erstaviksbadet (3km/2mi).

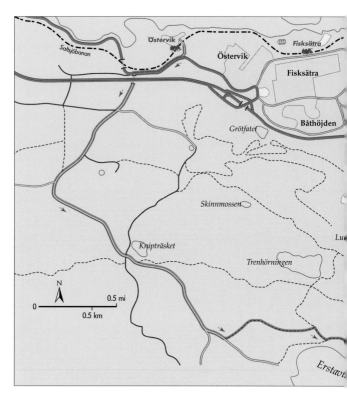

the right, about 100m/yds further on you come to a **blue sign** pointing to 'Erstaviksbadet'. Go left here, on a narrow but easily followed path through the woods. After about 1km/0.6mi, at a T-junction, go right. Now the path begins its descent towards Erstaviksbadet. Just after another sign for Erstaviksbadet, the

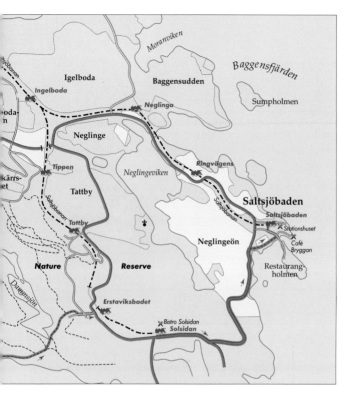

path forks: take the smaller path down to the right (although it really doesn't matter if you take the one to the left, as they rejoin later).

After a brief descent, you reach the water of **Erstaviken**, with good views and, a little further on, a **beach**. Depending on

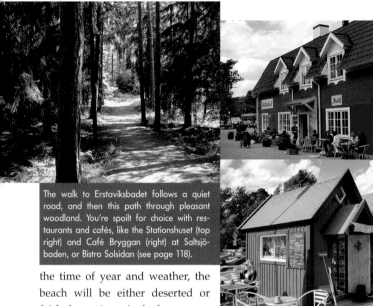

The walk to Erstaviksbadet follows a quiet road, and then this path through pleasant woodland. You're spoilt for choice with restaurants and cafés, like the Stationshuset (top right) and Café Bryggan (right) at Saltsjöbaden, or Bistro Solsidan (see page 118).

the time of year and weather, the beach will be either deserted or fairly busy. Amazingly for an area where relatively few people go, there is a simple café hidden behind trees at the top of the slope directly behind the beach.

From the beach or kiosk, rejoin the main path which runs by the water above the rocks near the water's edge. This is a popular area for picnics. The path slowly veers away from the water until you come to a junction marked with a wooden sign, '**Naturreserverat**', where you follow the path to the left. This leads into one of the most beautiful parts of the walk, as you cross a small wooden bridge with a lake, **Dammsjön**, to your left. After about five minutes the path emerges at a car park;

cross this and follow the car park access road out to a main road. Cross over and take the short path to **Erstaviksbadet station**. All trains stop here (although it is a request stop very early in the morning and late at night).

While you could take the train from Erstaviksbadet straight back to Slussen, changing at Igelboda (all trains are timed to connect), it is much more pleasant to take it to **Solsidan**, perhaps have lunch at the bistro described overleaf) and then walk on to Saltsjöbaden (from Solsidan station, just follow the road —

The Saltsjöbanan railway, which runs east from Slussen, is worth a trip in itself. Built in 1893, many of the wooden-platformed stations retain their original features. Some, such as Östervik and Erstaviksbadet (shown above), are very lightly used. There are many possibilities for walks based on the railway. It's also worth taking the train on to the terminus at Saltsjöbaden, or the branch line terminus at Solsidan (one stop from Erstaviksbadet or a five-minute walk).

Skyttevägen, Rosundsavägen and then the Saltsjöpromanaden past the harbour to **Saltsjöbaden station**).

Saltsjöbaden is worth lingering in for a while. The resort, with the Grand Hotel Saltsjöbaden as its centrepiece, was built by wealthy Knut A Wallenberg in 1891, who also built the Saltsjöbanan railway to serve it. There is a café, Stationshuset, that sells very good organic lunches and snacks. In summer, sit out by little Café Bryggan in a peaceful spot at the harbour and enjoy their delicious cinnamon buns.

Bistro Solsidan

Finding true 'dagens lunch' (see page 25) outside the city is not always easy: Bistro Solsidan is an exception. Situated in the former station house at Solsidan, the restaurant is a one-minute train ride from Erstaviksbadet or a five-minute walk.

Lunch is a steal at 65kr, including salad, soft drink and coffee or tea. There is usually one meat, one fish and one pasta dish daily. The surroundings are in keeping with the railway theme, with local memorabilia and photographs. To sit by the window on the railway side and watch the trains trundle in and out as you eat is like stepping back into a calmer age. During the evening the prices step up — but not too sharply — as does the choice.

The wine list is Italian and Spanish-themed, including the high-class, rich-red Museum Real Reserva. Jazz music nights are held every second Wednesday, and the trains run back to Stockholm long after closing time!

BISTRO SOLSIDAN
Bistro Solsidan. Skyttevägen 16, Solsidan (08 717 04 55. Open Mon-Fri 09.30-22.00, Sat-Sun 12.00-22.00. £ Lunch, £-££ dinner.

Lunch: changes daily, choice of three dishes every day. Dinner: meat-oriented, with grilled, entrecote, meatballs, beef. Fish: potato-baked salmon in mushroom sauce with grilled spring onions. Dessert: white chocolate panna cotta with summer berries.

restaurants

eat

PYTT I PANNA

Pytt i panna is a classic Swedish hash. Since it originated as a dish to use up leftovers, it's unlikely you'll find it on restaurant dinner menus — but it retains its status as a 'classic' lunch dish.

Traditionally *pytt i panna* was made with meat leftovers, but modern versions include fish and vegetarian versions. So adapt this recipe as you like.

Cut the potatoes into small cubes and boil until almost done but still fairly hard. If not already in pieces, cut the meat/fish into small bits. Chop the onion and fry with the meat/fish/vegetarian meat until the contents are cooked through, then remove from pan.

Put the potatoes in the pan and fry until golden brown. Sprinkle with salt and pepper. Add the meat/fish/onions to the potatoes and mix well. At the same time, fry the four eggs.

Serve with one egg on top of each portion and with the beetroot as an optional side dish.

Ingredients (for 4 people)

300 g leftover meat/fish of your choice OR
300 g salmon fillets OR
300 g vegetarian meat substitute of your choice (to make a vegetarian *pytt*)
2 medium-sized onions
750 g potatoes (about 8-10 medium potatoes)
1 tsp salt
1 dash pepper
4 free-range/organic eggs
1 jar beetroot (optional)
cooking margarine

recipes

eat

This easy walk around the village of Tyresö is suitable for any time of the year, and is a good introduction to Swedish village life — including some unusual sights! If you plan to visit the castle, note that it is only open on weekends in summer, and only for guided tours.

tyresö slott

WALK

10

The bus stops at **Tyresö** *kyrka* (church); first built in 1641, it is Gothic in style. An unusual feature is its truncated spire — the tower was not rebuilt after a fire in 1790 destroyed the church. From the **bus stop**, walk in the opposite direction from the departing bus, following the path signposted for Tyresö Slott and Notholmen. Beyond a gate, where the castle towers above you to the left, you are in the **castle gardens**, created in 1770 and the first English-style gardens to be opened in Sweden. There are many open spaces and benches to rest or picnic. Before long, you come to a bridge over to the small island of **Notholmen**, where you will find Café Notholmen — a very popular spot, which can be crowded in summer.

Distance: 5.3km/3.3mi; 2h30min

Grade: easy, all year round walk; very easy to follow walk on well-maintained paths with few gradients

Equipment: see pages 10-12; sun protection

Transport: 🚌 or **U** green line from Centralen to Gullmarsplan (journey time 9min), then 🚌 875 to Tyresö (journey time 30min; buses every 20min). Alight at the church (*kyrka*).

Refreshments: at the start (Café Notholmen) and midway (various in the village square)

Points of interest:
Tyresö church (*kyrka*)
Tyresö Castle and park
Notholmen island and café
Snusbullraeken (old shop in a tree)
Sculptures in Tyresö

Shorter walk: Tyresö church and castle area only (2.8km/1.7m)

Tyresö Slott; the castle is surounded by lovely English-style gardens.

Re-crossing the bridge to the mainland, follow the main path to the right, through the woodland to the rear of the castle. When you reach the **greenhouses** on the right, take the path to the left, cross another **bridge**, and head up towards the castle. At the top of this slope there are some lovely secluded seats set around a sculpture. Heading away from here, you will see a gap where you can walk around to the front of **Tyresö Slott**. Built in the mid-17th century, the castle is open to the public in summer (guided tours only; Sat/Sun from early

You cannot fail to notice this very unusual tree on the right-hand side of Kyrkvägen! This is *Snusbullraeken*, a tree which used to have a hole in the bottom where an old lady ran a shop selling *snus* (snuff — still very popular in Sweden) and sweets to passers-by. The shop even had a door, but it was blocked up with cement in 1929...

May to the beginning of July, *Sun only* from the beginning of July until the end of September; tours at 12 noon, 1pm, 2pm).

From the castle, follow the slope down to the right, back towards the church, and walk past the bus stop where you started out, keeping it to your right. Walk straight up Kyrk-vägen — there is no footpath, but there is not much traffic on this road. Continue on Kyrkvägen as far as Apelvägen, then turn left and follow this quiet road through some fine examples of typical Swedish family houses. At the end of the road, turn

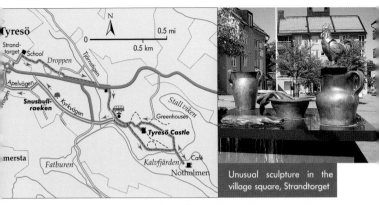

Unusual sculpture in the village square, Strandtorget

right downhill on Prästgårdsvägen. At the bottom, take the pedestrian underpass and go forwards into **Strandtorget**.

This is a typical suburban square, with shops, cafés and a couple of simple restaurants — although it does have an unusual bronze sculpture as its centrepiece. Walk across the square and leave at the right-hand side — heading towards the school buildings straight ahead (where there is another fine sculpture of two swans). Turn right alongside the school, right again at the end of the building, and then immediately left on a path through a small park. To the right you pass **Droppen**, a pond with a miniature summer cottage floating in the middle!

Follow the path as it joins the main road and, ignoring the signs indicating Tyresö Slott to the right, keep ahead past Tjärnstigen on your left. When you reach an isolated shop on the right, turn right on a path just behind it; this leads back to **Tyresö** *kyrka* and the **bus stop**.

Café Notholmen

A lovely little 'summer café' on the small island of Notholmen, connected by a bridge to the grounds of Tyresö Slott. The café offers traditional Swedish snacks and light lunches.

There is a large outdoor area around the café, so it's easy to find a quiet spot. You can drop by for a coffee or while away the whole afternoon sitting by the water.

Of course cinnamon buns are on offer, too! Swedes love their cakes and buns! If you visit a Swedish home at any time of the day you may well be invited to take a *fika* — that is, to take coffee, usually with assorted buns. These can be a selection of biscuits, cakes or the classic Swedish cinnamon bun *(kanelbullar)*. You'll find them on sale in every bakery, supermarket and in most cafés, but they are easy to make — see recipe opposite.

CAFÉ NOTHOLMEN
Slottsvägen, Tyresö. (08 770 35 50
www.cafenotholmen.se (only in Swedish, but plenty of photos, including the dishes served). Open daily in May from 10.00-16.00, in Jun/Jul/Aug Jun from 09.00-18.00, and in Sep from 10.00-16.00. Open on weekends the rest of the year.

sandwiches — speciality herring sandwich; also ham and cheese, meatballs, prawn

salads and pies

soups in winter

snacks and sweets, including raspberry and apple pie with vanilla sauce

restaurants

eat

SWEDISH CINNAMON BUNS

If you make up a quantity, don't worry — some can be frozen and defrosted in the microwave when a *fika* beckons!

Preheat the oven to 220°C, 425°F, gas mark 7.

Warm the milk to lukewarm, crumble in the yeast and stir until the yeast dissolves. Melt 120 g of the butter and mix in. Add the flour, 100 g of sugar, salt, cardemom and one egg and mix thoroughly.

Knead the dough for about 5 min, cover with a cloth and let it rise for 30-40 min. In the meantime, beat the remaining egg with a couple of tablespoons of water.

Roll out the dough into a long flat strip, around 3 mm thick and 30 cm wide. Melt the remaining butter so it is spreadable and brush it over the top of the dough. Mix the cinnamon and remaining sugar and sprinkle evenly on top. Roll up the dough lengthwise into a long roll and cut into 25 pieces. Place the cut pieces in paper moulds. Cover them with the cloth and let them rise again until they have doubled in size.

Brush the egg/water mixture on top of the buns and sprinkle pearl sugar on top. Bake in the middle of the oven for around 6 min, then cool. Serve with coffee, tea or hot chocolate.

Assorted cakes, biscuits and cinnamon buns for a *fika*

<u>Ingredients (for 25 buns)</u>
750 g flour
150 g sugar
300 ml milk
220 g butter
2 eggs
1 tsp salt
1 tbs ground cardemom
35 g yeast
2 tbs cinammon
pearl sugar

recipes

eat

This woodland walk from the village of Tyresta to Handen is a good introduction to both the Tyresta National Park and the Sörmlandsleden described on page 134. You can explore primeval forest taking advantage of an extremely well marked route.

tyresta

WALK

11

Alighting from the bus at **Tyresta**, you will see the **national park's information centre** just a few metres away. Do pop in: the staff are friendly and helpful and have a huge resource of free leaflets (many in English), plus maps and books; there is also an exhibition about the Tyresta National Park.

A short walk south of the information centre is **Tyresta by** (Swedish for 'village') and stables. The small group of buildings is one of the best-preserved group of Swedish rural buildings in the Stockholm area. There is a simple café which is open most of the year, but beware: it usually closes for part of the summer! If it's closed, coffee is also available in the national park's information centre. Just

Distance: 8.5km/5.3mi; 3h30min

Grade: moderate (ascents/descents of 100m/300ft overall). Very well waymarked, but with many exposed tree roots and some waterlogging; good footwear is essential.

Equipment: see pages 10-12; walking sticks; sun protection

Transport: local 🚆 from Centralen to Handen (every 15min at peak times, every 30min off-peak; journey time 24min). At Handen take the exit at the rear of the train as you alight and follow signs to the bus terminal for 🚌 834 to Tyresta village (hourly; journey time 19min). Return by same 🚆 from Handen to Stockholm.

Refreshments: café at Tyresta village (start of the walk)

Points of interest:
Tyresta village
Tyresta National Park's information
  centre
Slätmossens Nature Park
Rudasjön lakes (photo page 134)

Shorter walks: several well-marked, shorter circular walks in the national park start and end in Tyresta.

outside the village, on the track from the information centre, there's a noticeboard with lots of information about walks, including the Sörmlandsleden (see page 134).

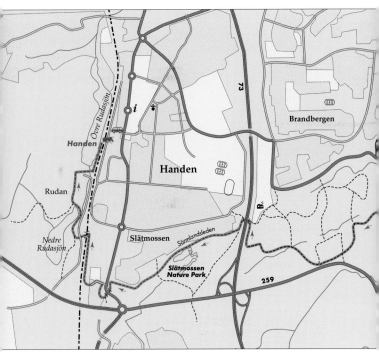

We are taking **Sörmlandsleden route number 4** back to
Handen, so follow the sign with the arrow, '**etapp 4**', walking
straight through the village. Leave the village at the left-hand
side, past a barbecue area and another sign, '**Handen 8**'. From
here the route is easily visible across a meadow; cross the small
wooden footbridge and head into the forest.

Once in the **forest** the path is very easy to follow, thanks to

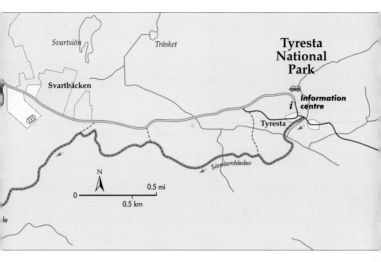

numerous red waymarks. Very quickly you enter beautiful, still primeval woods. After about 10 minutes you meet a vehicle track which is followed for about 50 m/yds before entering the forest again. As the path climbs, the real character of the national park becomes apparent. The pines grow amid lichen-covered, glacier-worn bedrock. The whole Tyresta area may look like a rolling landscape, but it is in fact an enormous shield of mountain bedrock that has fractured into several fissures. Within the fissures are many swamps and lakes. Above all, there are the giant Scots pines, some over 300 years old. Occasionally on the walk you come across clearings — but these are created by storms or fires, not by chopping, which is prohibited.

The path climbs past several **rocky outcrops**, good places to

Tyresta village; opposite: Slätmossen Nature Park

pause for a drink or snack. The outcrops are covered with lichen, mainly reindeer moss. After this the path descends again, rapidly. After around 45 minutes walking, a sign tells you that you are leaving the nature reserve. Ten minutes later the path joins a rough, vehicle-rutted track for a short stretch, then heads right, back into the forest.

A short way further along, the path forks: go left here for Handen, ignoring the route to Svartbacken. After another 25 minutes the path emerges by a **stable**. The Sörmlandsleden marking is still clear: walk past the stable and turn right, then go left through a very short stretch of forest. Meeting a road, cross over *carefully:* the traffic is very fast, and drivers will not be expecting you to emerge from the woods! The path continues on the far side of the road, slightly to the left. As it criss-crosses other tracks and paths, keep following the red waymarks. Soon you will hear a motorway in the distance and, as you near it, you come out on a tarmac path by a **power station**. Go left and take the underpass beneath the **motorway**. Then turn left and again follow the waymarking — into much more pleasant surroundings, with houses on your right and **Slätmossen Nature Park** to the left.

When you reach a road, follow the path to the left and take the underpass. Then swing right towards a petrol station. Turn left along Anna Marias Vägen, after which the route becomes

woodland track again. Follow the trail for about 10 minutes, with the **railway** to your left, until you reach a large **footbridge** that takes you over the railway. From the bridge, looking right, you can see the pink building of Handen station in the near distance. Over the bridge, turn right towards Handen. The path runs to the right of the open-air area of **Rudan**, with its two lakes — a very popular spot for locals to picnic, play, stroll and sunbathe. Walking straight along, with the railway on your right, you soon arrive back at **Handen station**.

SWEDISH ALCOHOLIC DRINKS

Swedish beer, often the butt of cruel jokes, is on the way back. It's true that many beer drinkers still order a standard *stor stark* (literally 'big strong') or simply *öl* (beer). A wave of mergers and buy-outs among breweries in the 1970s and 1980s led to dominance by three big conglomerates: Pripps, Spendrups and Falcon. This in turn led to a preponderance of easy-to-drink, characterless lagers.

But small breweries came back from the edge of extinction and the beer choice in Sweden is now better than ever. True, in many restaurants and bars you'll still just get lager from the 'big three', but specialist brews are becoming more common, and the choice in the Systembolaget (see page 20) is very broad. The big breweries have also responded by upping their own quality with some interesting bottled brews.

In Stockholm, the **Nils Oscar Brewery**, founded in 1996, has its own pub at Sankt Eriksgatan 36 (Fridhemsplan underground station), while on Södermalm, **Akkurat**, at Hornsgatan 18 (Slussen underground station) is a beer-lover's haven.

Sweet cider is also common, fermented from apples or pears.

With Sweden part of the spirit belt, distilled spirits are common, and are often drunk as appetisers or to accompany festive meals, such as Christmas and midsummer. If you attend such an event, be prepared for lots of toasts followed by emptying the spirit glass in one shot: beware not to get carried away — literally!

For a digestif, try a Swedish *punsch* — a sweet liquor with around 26% alcohol, that can be drunk with coffee or as an accompaniment to cheese.

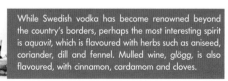

While Swedish vodka has become renowned beyond the country's borders, perhaps the most interesting spirit is *aquavit*, which is flavoured with herbs such as aniseed, coriander, dill and fennel. Mulled wine, *glögg*, is also flavoured, with cinnamon, cardamom and cloves.

Kvarnen

Kvarnen is a must-see on any visit to Stockholm — one of the few surviving traditional Swedish beer halls. Nowadays updated to include a lively back room with DJs, the main hall still retains its traditional charm with lots of wood panelling. Kvarnen has long been associated with Stockholm's radical left, and although its image has been considerably softened, it is still the meeting place for poets, musicians and outsiders. To get there, take the underground green line to Medborgarplatsen and leave by the exit in the middle of the platform (see town plan).

BAR/RESTAURANT KVARNEN
Tjärhovsgatan 4, Stockholm. (08 643 03 80. Open Mon-Fri 11.00-03.00; Sat 12.00-03.00; Sun 17.00-03.00. £-££

great value lunches (11.00-14.00 Mon-Fri): **two dishes of the day** (changes daily) at 75kr; selection of other **dishes of the week** from 75kr-105kr. **These menus specialise** in Swedish classic dishes — *pytt i panna*; fried herring with caviar, crème fraîche and boiled potatoes; homemade meatballs with mashed potato. All dishes include soft drink or light beer, home-made bread, salad and tea or coffee.

evening meals also at very reasonable prices:
8 entrées, including chanterelle mushroom soup with Västerbotten cheese; four different types of herring *(sill)* served with cheeses

around **12 different mains**, ranging from *pytt i panna* to pork fillets with saffron risotto or fried flounder with grilled beetroot and potato purée.

5 desserts (served in small portions; have one, three, four or all five!) —like apple pie with custard, white chocolate cheesecake or mint chocolate brulée

---

restaurants

eat

Sörmlandsleden is a network of paths in the county of Sörmland, extending over 1000km/620mi and divided into around 100 sections. The paths are extremely well signposted and waymarked and offer an ideal way for visitors to Stockholm to experience slightly more testing walks and a real taste of the Swedish wilderness.

sörmlandsleden

WALK

About 15 of the walks are south or southwest of central Stockholm, while others are much further to the south and west, around the towns of Nyköping, Katrineholm and Eskilstuna. For an **outline map** see www.sormlandsleden.se, where **stages of the walk are numbered** (and there is plentiful information in English).

If you did walk Walk 11 from Tyresta, you have already followed one of the stages (number 4) and will have seen how well marked the paths are — with frequent orange stripes encircling trees or poles, signs with 'Sörmlandsleden' and arrows with 'S'. In places, there is also blue

Transport: The Sörmlandsleden can be picked up and left at several points on the Stockholms Lokaltrafik network. Here are seven suggestions for sections that can be easily reached from the Stockholm area by underground (**U**), Bus (🚌) or train (🚈).

Numbers at the left refer to the Sörmlandsleden numbering of walk stages — see the outline map on their web site, mentioned left.

1 between **Björkhagen** (**U**) and **Skogshyddan** (🚌): 8km/6mi

2 between **Skogshyddan** (🚌) and the **Alby recreation centre** (🚌): 6km/3.7mi

3 between the **Alby recreation centre** (🚌) and **Tyresta village** (🚌): 12km/7.5mi

4 between **Tyresta village** (🚌) and **Handen** (🚈): 8.5km/5.3mi *(Walk 11 in this book)*

5:1 between **Kvarnängens sports ground** at Nynäshamn (🚈) and **Vansta sports ground** at Ösmo (🚈): 9.5km/6mi

5:2 between **Vansta**, Ösmo (🚈) and **Hemfosa** (🚈): 14km/8.7mi

6:1+6 between **Huddinge station** (🚌/🚈) and **Lida** (🚌): 20km/12.4mi

Sameslingan 5,0

0,6

waymarking, indicating that the section is also part of a shorter circular route. Planks and footbridges take walkers across difficult and water-logged areas. Signs with maps are in place at the start of each stage.

As the paths are extremely well waymarked, it is almost impossible to get lost. Nevertheless, there are plenty of ascents and descents, and quite rough paths with many exposed tree roots. These are definitely *not* walks to try in winter without expert local guidance, as some routes may be impassable and waymarkers obscured by snow.

There are shelters and a number of youth hostels or similar accommodation on some of the routes, but long-distance walkers are recommended to bring tents, as the paths sometimes go through long stretches of uninhabited countryside with no access to other accommodation. It is also vital to bring *plentiful water and other supplies* — there are some wells, but also long stretches with no access to fresh water or food.

Björnö Nature Reserve

Another idea for a great day out is a visit to the Björnö Nature Reserve on the island of Ingarö (see excursion map on page 102). It can be reached by bus 428/429 from Slussen in just 1h.

It's best to alight at Björkvik's Gård (one stop short of the terminus), then the entrance to the reserve is just to the left, by the bus stop.

It's a very popular place for camping; facilities are numerous and well maintained. There is a simple café at Björkvik and good beaches.

For a map of the reserve go to the Stockholm Archipelago web site, www.skargardsstiftelsen.se, and click on Björnö on the English pages. There are many more superb ideas for excursions and/or camping on the site.

Food intolerances are becoming ever more common, and we know there are a lot of you out there. Even if you have learned to cope at home, it can be very daunting to go on holiday. Will the food in restaurants be safe? Will I be able to buy gluten- and dairy-free foods?

In Sweden there is a high awareness of gluten and dairy-free diets, so you can buy ingredients without any worries.

Eating in restaurants

The more 'up-market' establishments may offer gluten-free breads, but the best bet is to bring your own, readily available in Stockholm supermarkets.

In the run-of-the-mill 'dagens lunch' establishments, the food is often prepared in advance — 'canteen food' for quick, economic serving; this is one reason why they are so cheap; so *beware.* It's very unlikely that they will interrupt their lunchtime rush to cook up a gluten-free alternative for you. But in higher-class restaurants, such as Gondolen, where the meals are, of course, prepared individually whatever the time of day, you will be on much safer ground.

Dinner in restaurants should present no such problems, but please explain clearly what your requirements are. Although the standard of spoken English is among the highest in Europe, don't let your guard down. Yes, Swedes might be able to speak English as if they were natives, but this

EAT GF, DF

doesn't mean they'll grasp idiomatic usage. Saying 'Is it dairy-free?' could easily lead to misunderstandings! You need to spell out: does it contain wheat products, milk, cream and so on. The ingredient decoder on pages 139-142 should help you to do this.

Gf, df shopping

All the major supermarkets have gluten-free and dairy-free sections, so you will be spoilt for choice. Semper and Finax are among the major producers, but there are many more. Bread, both hard and soft, gluten-free cakes and biscuits, and muesli can all be bought, as can gluten-free bread and cake mixes. Gluten-free pasta is readily available.

Soya milks and other milk alternatives are wide ranging — natural, chocolate- or banana-flavoured. There's also a good selection of soya yoghurts and creams.

CONVERSION TABLES

Weights		Volume		Oven temperatures		
						gas
				°C	°F	mark
10 g	1/2 oz	15 ml	1 tbsp	140°C	275°F	1
25 g	1 oz	55 ml	2 fl oz	150°C	300°F	2
50 g	2 oz	75 ml	3 fl oz	170°C	325°F	3
110 g	4 oz	150 ml	1/4 pt	180°C	350°F	4
200 g	7 oz	275 ml	1/2 pt	190°C	375°F	5
350 g	12 oz	570 ml	1 pt	200°C	400°F	6
450 g	1 lb	1 l	1-3/4 pt	220°C	425°F	7
700 g	1 lb 8 oz	1.5 l	2-1/2 pt	230°C	430°F	8
900 g	2 lb			240°C	475°F	9
1.35 kg	3 lb					

gf contains/may contain or be contaminated with gluten; lf contains/may contain lactose

Menu decoder/ Ingredients list for shopping
(see also 'Food preparation' inside the back cover)

abborre perch

ägg egg

ål eel

älgstek reindeer steak

amarantmjöl amaranth flour *gf*

ananas pineapple

ängsyra sorrel

anka duck

ansjovis anchovy

apelsin orange

äpple apple
 kaka tart *gf*
 paj pie *gf*

aprikos apricot

aquavit see page 132

arrowrot arrowroot

ärtor peas

ärtsoppa pea soup, *NB:* usually includes pieces of pork

ättika vinegar

avokado avocado

bakelse piece of cake *gf lf*

banan banana

basilika basil

betfiber beet fibre

biff steak

bikarbonat baking soda *gf*

björnbär blackberry

blåbär bilberry

blandsallad mixed salad

[blek]selleri celery

blomkål cauliflower

böckling smoked baltic herring

bönor beans

bovetemjöl buckwheat flour *gf*

braxen bream

bröd bread *gf lf*

bruna bönor brown beans

brysselkål brussel sprouts

bulgur bulgur wheat *gf*

buljong bouillon *lf*

bulle bun *gf lf*

carob carob

cashewnötter cashew nuts

champinjoner mushrooms

chilipulver chili powder

chips potato crisps *lf*

chocklad chocolate *lf*

citron lemon

citrongräs lemon grass

dinkelvete spelt *gf*

dragon tarragon

durumvete durum wheat *gf*

duva pigeon

E-nr (alla) E-numbers (all)

emulgeringsmedel emulsifier

enbär juniper berries

entrecôte prime rib

enzymer enzymes

fågel poultry

fänkål fennel

farin brown sugar

fårmjölk sheep's milk *lf*

fårost ewe's milk cheese *lf*

färskost goat's cheese *lf*

färska räkor unshelled prawns

fett fat
 animaliskt animal
 vegetabiliskt vegetable

filé fillet

filmjölk processed sour milk *lf*

fisk fish

fisksoppa fish soup

fläsk pork

flingor breakfast cereal *gf lf*

forell trout

förtjockningsmedel thickening agent (of fruit seeds)

frukter fruits

fruktjuice fruit juice

fruktkärnmjöl carob bean based thickening agent

fruktsallad fruit salad

fullkorns wholegrain
 mjöl flour *gf*
 ris rice

gädda pike

gås goose

gelé jelly

get goat
 mjölk milk *lf*
 ost cheese *lf*

glass ice cream *lf*

glögg mulled wine

glukos glucose

glutamat glutamate

gös pike-perch

grädde cream *lf*

gräddfil soured cream

gräddpulver cream powder *lf*

grahamsmjöl wholegrain wheat flour *gf*

grapefrukt grapefruit

gräslök chives

gravlax marinated salmon

grodd wheatgerm *gf*

GLOSSARY

gf contains/may contain or be contaminated with gluten; df contains/may contain lactose

grönkål green cabbage

grönsaker vegetables

grönsallad green salad/lettuce

gröt porridge gf df

gryta stew gf df

guarkärnmjöl guar flour

guargum guar gum

gurka cucumber

gurkmeja turmeric

hallon raspberries

hamburgare hamburger gf

hasselnötter hazelnuts

havre oats gf

havrekli oat bran gf

havremjöl oat flour gf

havsabborre sea bass

havskräftor scampi

helgeflundra halibut

helkornsmjöl wholegrain flour

hirs millet

hjortron cloudberries

hön hen

honung honey

hovmästarsås dill sauce

hummer lobster

idealmjöl thickening agent gf

ingefära ginger

isglass ice lollies df

ister lard

jamsmjöl type of g-f flour

Janssons frestelse see page 41

johannesbröd-kärnmjöl carob bean thickening agent

jordgubbar strawberries

jordnötter peanuts

julbord Christmas buffet gf df

kabeljo salted cod

kaffe coffee

kakao cocoa

  massa mass

  mör butter

  pulver powder

kål cabbage

kalkon turkey

kålrötter turnips

kalvkotlett veal chops

kamutvete kamut flour gf

kanel cinnamon

kantareller chanterelle mushrooms

kapris capers

kardemumma cardamom

kärnmjölkspulver buttermilk df

karp carp

kastanjemjöl chestnut flour

kefir yoghurt-type sour milk df

kesella fresh cheese similar to ricotta df

keso cottage cheese df

kex biscuits gf df

kikärter chickpeas

klumpförebyg-gande medel anti-caking agent

kokos coconut

  mjölk milk

kolja haddock

konserveringsmedel preservative

koriander coriander

korn barley gf

  mjöl flour gf

körsbär cherries

korv sausages gf

kostfiber fibre gf

kotlett meat chops

köttbullar meatballs gf df

köttfärs beef mince

krabba crab

kräfta crayfish

kronärtskockor artichokes

kroppkakor potato dumplings, filled with bacon and onions gf df

krusbär gooseberries

kryddor herbs and spices

kummel hake

kumminfrö caraway seeds

kvarg fresh cheese made from sour milk df

kyckling chicken

lagerblad bay leaves

lägg hock

lake burbot

lakritsgodis liquorice candy gf

laktos lactose df

lamm lamb

lantbrödsmjöl rich wheat flour gf

läsk soft drink

lax salmon

lever liver

linser lentils

löjrom bleak roe

lök onion

  rostad lök roasted onion gf (may have been roasted with flour)

löpe rennet df

lupinmjöl lupin flour

lutfisk stockfish

majsmjöl cornflour

makaroner macaroni gf

makrill mackerel

malt malt gf

  arom flavour gf

  extrakt extract gf

  sirap syrup gf

maltodextrin maltodextrin, used as a food binder

maltos maltose gf

manitoba vete manitoba flour gf

mannagryn semolina gf

maräng meringue

gf contains/may contain or be contaminated with gluten; *df* contains/may contain lactose

margarin margarine *df*

ost cheese *df*

marmelad marmalade

marulk monkfish

matvete wheat grains *gf*

mazarin almond tart *gf* & *df*

med kolsyra carbonated (soft drink or water)

mejram marjoram

mellanfransyskan rump steak

mesost sweet goat cheese from northern Sweden *df*

messmör spreadable goat cheese from northern Sweden *df*

mjukost soft cheese *df*

mineralvatten mineral water

mjöl flour
  amarant amaranth flour *gf*
  bovete buckwheat *gf*
  grahams wholegrain wheat *gf*
  guarkärn guar flour
  havre oat *gf*
  helkorns wholegrain *gf*
  jams type of g-f flour
  kastanje chestnut flour

korn barley *gf*

lantbröds rich wheat *gf*

lupin lupin flour

majs corn

potatis potatoes

quinoa quinoa *gf*

råg rye *gf*

sikt rye flour mixed with wheat flour *gf*

skrädmjöl toasted oat *gf*

sojabönor soya bean

sorghum sorghum

tarakärn type of g-f flour

teff g-f flour made from a type of African grass

vete wheat *gf*

mjölbehandlingsmedel flour treatment agent

mjölk milk *df*
  albumin albumin *df*
  kärn buttermilk *df*
  protein protein *df*
  pulver powder
  skum skimmed
  socker sugar
  steril sterilised
  syra lactic acid *df*
  torr powdered

modifierad stärkelse modified starch *gf*

morötter carrots

mört roach (a carp-like fish)

mousserande vin sparkling wine

munk donut *gf* & *df*

muskot nutmeg

mynta mint

natriumkaseinat milk protein

nejlikor cloves

nektarin nectarine

nudlar noodles *gf*

öl beer *gf*

oliver olives

olja oil
  vegetabilisk vegetable

omelette omelette *df*

oregano oregano

ost cheese *df*

ostkaka cheese curd cake *gf*

ostkex cheese crackers *gf* & *df*

ostron oysters

paj pie *gf*

palsternacka parsnip

pannkaka pancakes *gf* & *df*

paprika peppers (red/green/yellow)

päron pear

passionsfrukt passion fruit

pektin pectin

pepparkakor ginger biscuits *gf* & *df*

pepparmynta peppermint

pepparrot horseradish

persika peach

persilja parsley

piggvar turbot

pinjekärnor pine nuts

pittabröd pitta bread *gf*

plommon plum

polentagryn polenta grain

potatis potatoes
  fiber fiber
  mjöl flour

sallad salad *df*

pumpa pumpkin

punsch sweet liqueur

purjolök leek

pytt i panna see page 119

quinoamjöl quinoa flour *gf*

rabarber rhubarb

rädisor radishes

råg rye *gf*
  kross crushed *gf*
  mjöl flour *gf*
  sikt rye flour mixed with wheat flour *gf*

räkor prawns

regnbågsforell rainbow trout

revbensspjäll spare ribs *gf*

rimmad lax lightly salted raw salmon

rimmat fläsk salt-cured pork

ris rice
  dryck drink

röda vinbär red-currants

gf contains/may contain or be contaminated with gluten; *df* contains/may contain lactose

rödbetor beetroot

röding char

rödkål red cabbage

rödspätta plaice

rödtunga witch flounder

rökt lax smoked salmon

rosmarin rosemary

rostat bröd toast *gf*

rotselleri celery root

russin raisins

saffran saffron

saffransbulle saffron bun *gf df*

saft still cordial drink

sagogryn sago grains

salvia sage

sardiner sardines

schalottenlök shallot

sellerisalt celery salt

senapsfrö mustard seed

senapspulver mustard powder

sesamfrö sesame seed

sik whitefish

sill herring

sillbricka variety of marinated herring

sjötunga sole

skaldjur shellfish

skärbönor string beans

skinka ham

skogshönsfågel grouse

skorpsmulor crisp-roll crumbs *gf*

skrädmjöl toasted oat flour *gf*

släpärter peas in the pod

slätvar brill

smör butter *df*

smörgåsbord large buffet *gf df*

sniglar snails

socker sugar

sockerärter sugar peas

sockerdricka lemonade

sojabönor soya bean

  dryck drink

  mjöl flour

sojasås soy sauce *gf*

sorbet sorbet *df*

sorghummjöl sorghum flour

sparris asparagus

speltvete spelt flour mixed with wheat flour *gf*

spenat spinach

spiskummin cumin

stärkelse starch

  blekt bleached

  majsmjöl cornflour

  modifierad modified *gf*

  oxiderad oxidised

  sirap syrup

  vete wheat *gf*

stärkelsesirap glucose syrup

stenbit lumpfish

ströbröd breadcrumbs *gf*

strömming fried herring (can be hot or cold)

surkål sauerkraut

surströmming see page 111

svagdricka see page 39

svartpeppar black pepper

sylt jam

syltlök pickled onions

tångräkor shrimps

tapioka tapioca

tarakärnmjöl type of g-f flour

te tea

teffmjöl g-f flour made from a type of African grass

timjan thyme

toast skagen toast with shrimp and bleak roe *gf*

tomat tomato

tonfisk tuna

torrmjölkspulver dried milk powder

torsk cod

tranbär cranberries

tunnbröd Swedish flat bread (see pages 78-79) *gf df*

utan kolsyra noncarbonated (soft drink or water)

våfflor waffles *gf df*

vallmofrö poppy seeds

vaniljsås custard *gf df*

varm chocklad hot chocolate *df*

varm korv hot dog

vassle whey *df*

Västerbottensost see pages 92-93

vatten water

vete wheat *gf*

  gräs grass *gf*

  groddolja wheat germ oil *gf*

  kli bran *gf*

  mjöl flour *gf*

  protein protein *gf*

sirap syrup *gf*

stärkelse starch *gf*

vin wine

vinäger vinegar

vindruvor grapes

vita bönor pea beans

vitkål white cabbage

vitling whiting

vitlök garlic

vitpeppar white pepper

wienerbröd Danish pastry *gf df*

yoghurt yoghurt *df*

zucchini courgettes

bold type: photograph; *italic type:* map

INDEX

First edition © 2008
Published by Sunflower Books
PO Box 36061, London SW7 3WS
www.sunflowerbooks.co.uk

ISBN 978-1-85691-350-8

Cover photograph: Riddarholmen from Södermalm
Photographs: front cover, 68 (bottom left), 88 © istock photo; 4 © Patrick Trägårdh, Swedish Institute, 21 © Richard Ryan, Swedish Institute; 41, 50, 62, 63, 125, 132 © Pål Allen, Swedish Institute; 49 © Hotel Rival; 60-61 © Gondolen; 64, 67 © Anke van Lenteren; 69 © Ulla Windblah; 98 (top), 99 (top) © Lotta Lind); 133 © Kvarnen; all others photographs © the author
Maps: Sunflower books, adapted from various sources (see page 13)
Series design: Jocelyn Lucas
Cookery editor: Marina Bayliss
A CIP catalogue record for this book is available from the British Library.
Printed and bound in China by WKT Company Ltd

Before you go ...
log on to
www.sunflowerbooks.co.uk
and click on '**updates**', to see if we have been notified of any changes to the routes or restaurants.

When you return ...
do let us know if any routes have changed because of road-building, storm damage or the like. Have any of our restaurants closed — or any new ones opened *on the route of the walk*? (Not Stockholm centre restaurants, please; these books are not intended to be complete restaurant guides!)
Send your comments to mail@sunflowerbooks.co.uk